I0539540

TABLE OF CONTENTS:

FOREWORD

CUT AWAY

CUT IT OUT

CUT THE CORD

CUT FOOTLOOSE

THE FIRST CUT IS THE DEEPEST

CUT THE CRAP

CUT ABOVE THE REST

CUTOFF SHORTS

CUT FROM THE SAME CLOTH

SHORTCUTS

CUT YOUR EGO OFF

CUT TO THE CHASE

LOVE IN THE CUT

DEDICATION

ABOUT THE AUTHOR

FOREWORD

Bitch Don't Cut Your Bangs was a labor of love and there are a few people I would love to thank. First, my editor, Kiersten. She's sunshine in human form and I could not have asked for a better person to edit my book. Wise beyond her years, with a heart full of love and acceptance. She just gets me; I knew when I first met her that she was special. I felt an instant soul connection and I knew I wanted to work with her on the journey of birthing this purposeful book. One of the things I discovered in writing my first chapter book is that an editor is invaluable. Kiersten is amazing, she's not only a talented writer and photographer but she is dedicated, thoughtful and hardworking. The editor we choose is of the utmost importance.

Working with Kiersten was a divine experience because she understood me, my heart, my process, my purpose. She was able to turn my thoughts and experiences, my rough drafts and scribbles into something I am so proud of. I am so proud of her; we made a pretty good team. I know my limitations and I was happy to hand the editing reins over to Kiersten so that she could work her magic. A great talent and a true friend, I am grateful that she took this journey with me. I especially appreciated that after she edited each chapter, she would send an encouraging message. That kept me motivated and excited. With all my heart, Kiersten, thank you for your expertise, your thoughtful insights, your kind words of encouragement and for all the BIG love. I've told you before and I'll say it again, "I adore you."

To my besties and you all know who you are. Bestie Debbie thank you for the idea of writing this book. Thank you to my besties Marylea, Carol, Francheska, Kim 1 and 2, Jess and anyone else I may have forgotten, for listening to me talk about this book and for the encouragement and support, for always being there to lift my spirits and remind me of my why. I am so grateful to have a group of amazing friends like you. I won the friendship lottery when I met each of you. You each inspire me with your stories, your strength and courage and more importantly with how you love and put up with a beautiful mess like me. Your fierce self-love and unconditional love for those around you inspired me to write this book. I am forever grateful.

To my special friend. Should you read this book, I wish to say thank you for all of it. For your valuable time, thank you for the memories, thank you for all the lessons you had no idea you were teaching me. Thank you for awakening this sleeping beauty and making me realize I was always capable of saving myself. That what I was seeking outside of myself, even from you, was within my own heart all along. I see that now. I hope you find that what you are searching for already exists inside you.

To my family. There is so much I could write at this point; however, I will keep it brief. I know that I have disappointed many of you and perhaps this book will only cause a further wedge between us. I don't know. I was called by Divine Spirit to write this book. If it can help even one other person feel safe, understood and loved then my efforts will not have been in vain. I am so sorry for all the hurt and pain I have caused you through my actions. Hindsight is 20/20 and the past is gone, and I cannot change it. I love you all so much and I will keep my light on for you, always. I am like a tree whose branches are open wide. You may stay or you may leave. Regardless of what you choose I will remain strong, growing, reaching, open, giving, receiving. My love for you is forever and always bigger than the world. To the family that has stood by me and loved me on my darkest days and carried me through the depths of my despair, thank you is not enough. I truly needed every ounce of unconditional love and support that only those who have known me my whole life could provide. I feel incredibly grateful for all of you.

Finally, to you the reader. I love you. You are loved and appreciated. I am grateful for the support. I hope you find this book useful if not for the insight that it holds at least for kindling your fireplace. Haha. Our life is our message. I hope together we can make it a beautiful one.

BIG love always,
Rebecca

CUT AWAY

I gave my power away to anyone and everyone who could make me feel loved. These feelings of love were my kryptonite. They were my greatest weakness and my eventual undoing. My desire for attention, which I equated with love, tricked me into forgetting my worth. These feelings are the main reason I cut my own bangs.

This reminds me of the story of Sampson and Delilah. If you are not familiar with the story, allow me to share it. Sampson was a man with supernatural strength. Upon his birth, he had been given this gift. However, his strength was connected to his hair. He was instructed to never cut or allow his hair to be cut. He was warned to never tell anyone the secret of his powerful strength. When he became a man, he was a warrior who could not be defeated, and this frustrated his enemies. Enter Delilah, a beautiful seductress who was hired by the opposing army, the enemy, to deceive Sampson. She did this by seducing him and making him fall in love with her. She earned his trust, and once Sampson had fallen for the "love" of the beautiful Delilah, he confessed his most sacred secret. He fell for the intoxicating feeling of love, which made him weak long before his hair was clipped. After Delilah learned of his secret, she cut his hair in the night. He had become powerless and lost his supernatural strength. He essentially gave his power away to earn the love of another. Seeking such love and validation outside of himself allowed him to be cut off from the source of his power and the source of the Divine Spirit itself. Well played, Delilah.

Often, we are our own worst enemies. I am living proof of this. I played myself without realizing it, which led me to make the horrific decision to cut my own bangs. This was just a culmination of many poor choices that I had made during that time in my life. I felt instant regret and began to question, Why? Why do any of us cut or alter our hair? This was a question I pondered, googled, and researched. It became very clear that there is a common thread—a theme of life-altering events—that influences us to take the scissors to our crown and glory. It's a theme that has played out in my own life.

After birthing each of my children, I made a dramatic change to my hair. I did it again, when switching careers and again through other life-changing moments. This instance was no different. I was craving a change. I had recently become an empty nester. I was feeling lonely, lost, and empty. I was looking for love in all the wrong places. While I was scrolling through social media, I saw a beautiful woman with gorgeous hair that I admired, and I noticed she had bangs. That's when I got the brilliant (or not so brilliant) idea to cut my own bangs. Surely, I thought this would brighten my mood and make me feel better. So I went into the kitchen, pulled out the orange-handled pair of scissors (you know the ones), went into the bathroom, stood in front of the mirror, and began snipping away at my hair. Immediately, I regretted my decision. You see, I have a cowlick, widows peak, and bangs have never laid right.

When I showed up the next day for a lunch date with two of my funniest girlfriends, one of them said, "What have you done? What made you cut bangs?" I shared what I was going through and told them how much regret I felt for doing the deed, and we all had a good laugh. That was the moment the idea for this book was conceived. You know what they say when life hands you lemons? Well, when life hands a little bitch a pair of kitchen scissors and she cuts her bangs, you write a book.

By sharing my story from empty to empowered and cut off to complete, I hope to connect with you. I hope you will join me on this journey as we create a life from love instead of for love. Ultimately, my greatest desire is that you would more deeply discover and connect with yourself, the power you possess, and the greatest love of your life—you!

CUT IT OUT

Powerful bitches cut out the doubt. They have dreams to chase and a purpose to fulfill. They don't have time to entertain fear and doubt. What excuses are we making that keep us from living a life beyond our wildest dreams? We all have excuses. Self-doubt is defeating, it is crippling, and it keeps us from reaching our full potential. Fear and doubt have got to go; cut them out like our lives depend on them. They are the cancer of the soul; nothing kills dreams faster than doubt. Fear and faith cannot occupy our thoughts at the same time.

We must choose faith over fear and doubt if we wish to step into our personal power and elevate ourselves to the highest version we can be. It is hard to be a doer when our heads are full of doubt. We second-guess ourselves, lose sight of our vision, get discouraged, and eventually give up. Doubt kills motivation; when we doubt, we forget we have the power to create our own lives. It is the number one thing that will hold us back from living the life that we desire. "If you have faith, even the size of a mustard seed, you can say to this mountain, "move," and it will move." We are powerful beings who possess within us the power to move the immovable.

"Nothing is impossible" is a quote I have in the entryway of my home. This is a quote that has always felt right to me. Although I do not use many quotes or sayings around my house as home décor, I did incorporate this one. Because I believe it, I feel it in every fiber of my being. We were designed to create the impossible. To prove to ourselves and others that there is an unexplainable mysterious connection to the creator of worlds, of Divine Spirits. That shit excites me. The creator of all things is a limitless force, and the Divine Spirit's expansiveness is unlimited. All things are possible in an ever-expanding world. Humans were in fact created by an energy force called love, created by dust from the earth, and the breath of the spirit of all creation was breathed into us. How can we then be limited in what we can become? We can't be; it's just a fact. We are co-creators and joint heirs to all that exists. The same spirit that raised a man from the dead lives in each of us as images of the divine. If we could grasp this and truly believe it, our lives would reflect the greatness of the Divine Spirit. Sadly, we doubt our abilities to tap into that limitless power that we are granted simply by existing. We stand in awe of others who create the most magnificent lives and call them lucky, or we label them geniuses. We place them on a pedestal and make an idol out of them. We label them our inspiration and dream of being one of them someday. What if I told you that we all have the Divine Spirit gene living inside of us? What if I told you we were one of them? Let's look at the biggest obstacle that keeps us from being our most empowered selves.

FEAR

Fear is what stands between where we are now, where we want to be, and who we want to be. Fear of rejection, fear of failure, fear of judgment, even fear of our own extraordinary abilities and success. How do we conquer fear? We face it! Armed with faith in ourselves and a higher power that fuels our self-confidence, I believe we can conquer anything. Even delusional thoughts of fear and doubt will fade. The best way to face fear and doubt is by taking action.

Have you ever tried something new and experienced the discomfort of failure? As we age, this discomfort becomes less and less appealing. I believe this is one of the reasons we will choose to settle for a limited version of ourselves, because the discomfort and fear of the unknown seem worse to us than the discomfort of familiar security and predictability.

Being a child who was educationally challenged, fear of failure was beaten into me at an early age. I dreaded report card day and having to show it to my highly intelligent parents. I was a C-D student, barely passing most classes. I feared the feelings of shame associated with the disappointment of failure. The public school system, with its standardized education, was not a great fit for me. I struggled throughout most of my life with a fear of failure around my intellectual abilities. Due to my experiences, struggles, and conditioning as a child, I had never felt good enough or smart enough.

At an early age, I began hearing that I was stupid. My mother would often get frustrated with me when I needed help with my homework, and she would say to me, "Come on, you can't be that stupid." My peers and even a couple of teachers had called me dumb or stupid. One teacher my freshman year of high school called me dimwitted. She continued to tell me I would never amount to anything. That I would be a homemaker just like my mother (mind you, my mother was literally a genius and chose to be a homemaker). It wasn't for lack of trying either; I would follow along, take notes, and study. However, with each year and each blow to my self-esteem, fear of failure became a major mental block, creating a cycle of try-fear-fail. The fear of failing at even the simplest of school tasks or projects gave me crippling anxiety. The cycle began to turn around in my junior year of high school with the help of a very special English teacher.

This teacher looked beyond my poor grammar and misspellings to connect with the message of my story amongst the mess. She looked past the errors to find the heart of the poetry. She called me up to her desk one day—a conversation that would change my life. She told me I was a good writer. I had a gift for finding the right words to express my thoughts and painting a clear picture for the reader. I had the ability to pull the reader into my story and hold their attention. She told me that despite my poor grammar, I had talent in the area of creative writing. She told me she always looked forward to reading what I wrote. She encouraged me to write more and to not give up on my studies. She advised me, explaining that if I would turn in my work on time, do the extra credit, and keep doing my best, she would recommend me for an honors creative writing class for my senior year. This timely and divinely guided conversation was just the encouragement I needed to keep going. Pushing past the fear of failure and doubt day after day, I succeeded and was able to attend the advanced creative writing class. For the first time in my educational experience, I was successful. This is the power of words, and words have the power to disable fear and doubt. Words can be like weapons, and words can be like a healing salve for the soul. That is why I believe in the power of affirmations. This is the belief action to take to overcome fear of failure. We will not always have a teacher, famlly member, or friend to help us conquer our fear of failure. This is why we must learn to be our own heroes by affirming ourselves.

I don't fear failure like I used to. Maybe that's because I've had so much practice. Maybe it's because I am older and wiser, and I can see how failure is a necessary part of our story of success. After all, there are many individuals who overcame multiple failures and have made history in the most extraordinary ways. People who have conquered fear of failure, self-doubt, and the doubt of others have created worlds we all enjoy today. Disney World, Hogwarts, OZ, and Middle-Earth, just to name a few. If the Divine Spirit gave us a dream and the desire to fulfill a vision, we should not let fear of failure keep us from materializing this gift to the world. Let's instead believe that the power to create worlds is possible, and it is.

Fear of judgment, of looking foolish—how many of us can relate to not starting or not putting our full effort into something because we are afraid of what other people will think about us? Because that's all fear of looking foolish is—it's a fear of judgment. If we can learn to overcome our desire to be positively embraced at all times and accepted fully by others, we will be free.

I was intentionally on a mission to do just that. I felt the need to be as free as possible from the burden of the judgment of others. I had no idea, at the time, what would transpire from this experiment. Nor did I know what the exact process would look like, but what I did know was that I 100% wanted to do all of the things that I was scared to do, especially if it came to that fear of judgment. As a lifelong people-pleaser, I was desperate to break free from the shackles of others' perceptions of me. If the question "What will they think of me?" entered my mind, I was going to do it, and I was going to do it publicly, via social media, to ensure as many people could and would judge me. I was so determined to become immune to the judgments and criticism of others, to stop people-pleasing, and to stand in the fullness of my personal authentic power that I was willing to ruin my squeaky-clean reputation. I was so tired of my own emptiness, of living to please others and living up to their expectations of who they wanted me to be and who they believed me to be. I wanted to be free of others' perceptions of me. There's a quote on a cup I have that sums it up perfectly: "Once you have ruined your reputation, you can live quite freely." Anthony Bourdain.

I like to be naked in nature, alone. It's just a "thing" for me. It's not sexual in nature; it's just fun; it feels liberating; mostly, it feels natural. I have been taking my clothes off in nature for years just to feel that freedom. Most of the time, I'm just topless, but sometimes I like to take it all off and skinny dip in the ice-cold lake. It's invigorating. One day I went to the nature center a few miles from my house. I took my top and bra off and sat, with shorts on, on a large rock in the middle of a stream where it makes a tiny waterfall. I was resting my bare feet on the smaller rock below me. I had set up my tripod on the shore and began filming. I laughed and felt giddy with the innocence of it all. I looked younger, and I felt younger. My inner child was happy to be playing, and maybe my inner child was happy to be a bit naughty. I took more video footage of me fully clothed in nature, eating wild berries, holding hands with a leaf on a tree, and walking on a path. I heard the song Wild Things and thought, "This song is perfect." I created the reel for Instagram as I sat in the hot car at the end of my driveway. I chose to start the reel with the scene of me topless, with my long hair streaming down my back and me covering my naked breast with my arms. I titled it Rebecca Gone Wild. I typed out a motivational message about nature, added my hashtags, and sat there frozen with fear. "What will people think? What will they say? Will they think I am stupid, too old, or too much? What if my parents see it? You get the point. Finally, I said, "Fuck it" and hit "post." I knew my motive for posting wasn't for views or likes, although it did do well. I was posting to reveal my most authentic version of myself. I posted because I wanted to be free from the fear of the judgment of others. My goal was to build more confidence and empower myself. I would post many more of these provocative videos, embracing my body and free spirit. Several of them even went viral. With each video that I posted, I began to feel free of the need to perform for others' comfort, and I began to show up for myself in all my glory.

When we show up with a "fuck it" attitude toward judgment, we become a powerful force of energy. We become one with the source of energy that created us to embody our unique vibration. When our motives are clear and our intentions are pure, the Divine Spirit makes big moves on our behalf. A person who has the courage to show up and put themselves out there for the world to see will be judged, but they will also be rewarded. The action I took to overcome the fear of criticism and judgment from others was to just do it. Do it with fear; do it with uncertainty; do it with doubt; just do it. John Wooden said, "Be more concerned with your character than your reputation, because your character is what you really are, while your reputation is merely what others think you are."

I believe one of the greatest fears for all of us is the fear of rejection and/or abandonment. To feel that another person that we care about and love would not care about us or love us back. They would reject the most precious gift that we have to offer, the gift of our love and connection. We all have within us a natural desire to be loved and accepted. Rejection and abandonment are two of the most painful experiences one can have in life. We have all experienced the heartbreak of rejection and abandonment to some degree or another.

None of us was born immune to this experience. Most of us have had a breakup with either a romantic partner or a friendship. Some have been terminated from jobs, rejected by a child, sibling, parent, church organization, etc. Rejection and abandonment wounds are so painful that we will do almost anything to avoid this type of hurt, including choosing not to act at all. We will choose not to express our love; we will choose not to apply for that job; we will choose to stay in our comfort zones. How can we take action to free ourselves from this type of suffering? Since we cannot avoid rejection and abandonment in this human experience, we should build within ourselves a safe home. We must become so at peace with who we are that the absence of another person or thing does not disturb our peace. Furthermore, it is important that we do not reject or abandon ourselves. Should another person reject or abandon us, if we have built a strong sense of self-worth, we will not suffer as greatly compared to depending on another to provide that safety for us. When we build that home within another person who is not us (with Spirit), we will eventually suffer. Attachment is the root of all suffering. The truth is, no one stays forever. Loss is inevitable.

I used to fear rejection so much that I would turn myself inside out for other people. "Please don't leave me. Please choose me." I don't do that anymore. One of the most painful experiences I have had was when my adult children rejected having a relationship with me. If they had come to me during my weakest moments and my deepest sorrows over their decision, I would have agreed to become anyone or anything they wanted me to be to avoid ever feeling the pain of this loss. But I realize now that pain is a gift. When people reject us, they detach from us.

Unattachment is necessary for proper growth and healing to occur. This rejection was a redirection for me. It became a powerful turning point in my life and placed me on my own journey of healing and self-discovery. Just yesterday, I walked the block from my condo to the beach (I now live in Virginia Beach), and I stood in awe of the vastness of the ocean. My heart was full of gratitude for my new place. I thought to myself, "If I had not endured all of that suffering, I would have never known Virginia Beach. I may have never stood here and had the opportunity to experience this moment of contentment and peace, being one with the vastness of creation." Of course, I hope and pray for reunification with my beautiful children. Until then, I will continue to create a life for myself, anchoring myself in the Spirit as I become the most empowered version of myself I can be.

Here are the action steps I take to cut out fear of rejection and abandonment:.
1. I chose me. Instead of looking for others to choose me, I choose what I know to be in alignment with me and my purpose.
2. I build my self-worth by staying committed to my projects, goals, and commitments.
3. I create a safe home within myself through mindfulness, meditation, and education.

Fear and doubt are personal and manifest in many ways. I am just touching on a few common root fears. One of the most interesting fears that I am currently working to overcome is fear of personal success. In doing my research, I discovered that this is a common fear among humans. One of many reasons semi-successful people self-sabotage is to limit themselves to "good enough." Good is the enemy of the best. I have caught myself saying, "Aw, it's good enough." Instead of insisting on creating and giving my best, I will settle for "good enough." Once I was aware that I was saying this to myself, I spent some time reflecting on why we might say that.

I had gone for a run on the beach. I had a goal: I was going to run to the end of the beach until I ran out of land. I had no idea the exact distance. I just felt it was attainable, as I had walked most of it before (but had never walked all the way to the end). As I was running, I had the urge to keep looking back at this large landmark, the peer I started at. I would look far off into the distance to gauge how close I was to my goal while I was plodding along. Finally, Spirit interrupted my thoughts and said, Do not look back or you will say, "That's good enough. I've run far enough." Do not look too far ahead at the desired destination, or you will say, "That is too far. And I am afraid I am too tired to finish." You will fold under the pressure. Instead, keep your head up and your eyes on the path just in front of you, and then you are sure to reach your goal. Obviously, this is not just about running. If we set a goal and keep looking back to see how far we have come, we might become tempted to say, "That's good enough." If we look too far into the future, we may become discouraged by the distance and afraid that we do not have the strength, talent, or ability, and worst of all, that we will discover we were not chosen for this purpose and are unworthy of the life we imagined. It's this fear that will stop us in our tracks.

I admire people who have accomplished and achieved goals of influence, wealth, and success. I had never stopped to ponder the amount of pressure they must feel to maintain and grow their reputation, wealth, status, and success. I experienced some minor social media success, and after I had this experience, I had a different perspective on the fear of stepping into my own power and owning my authentic greatness, which we all possess. Now, I have had to manage my thoughts, attitude, emotions, and fear around personal success. "What if" and fear thoughts are new to me.

What if this is it? What if I've hit my peak potential? What if I run out of inspiration? What if I get too many subscribers? What if I don't get enough? What if I'm not doing this right? The fear and self-doubt I have felt some days have made me question, "Do I really need personal power to encourage others to step into theirs? I don't need to shine. I think I'll just hide away and go be a hermit in the mountains. Haha, those thoughts are no joke. You see, I feel so passionate about my calling and goals that I feel that if I cannot achieve them, I may as well run away and never be seen again. Dramatic, I know. So, I try to convince my performance-loving extraverted personality that being smaller and less than someone else would be better, safer, and less scary. The fear of owning our own power and being responsible for the purpose that comes with that is frightening. Fear of what if I succeed at this, I've discovered is truly rooted in fear of the unknown. If it makes us feel any better, nothing is guaranteed. Every new day brings the unknown. How do you want to step into the unknown? Are you afraid or empowered? Running the race that we have been called to run. Stepping into our souls' purpose requires us to step out of our comfort zone and get comfortable with the unknown. It requires us to face our fears and keep moving despite the discomfort. I continue to push myself beyond the limits of fear and doubt. I am choosing to do things that I have judged and might be considered morally questionable within our society. I do it consciously, knowing that as I face these fears of judgment, rejection, and success, I am becoming a more empowered human.

I would love to encourage everyone to seek out all the fear that exists in our beings and begin to challenge it so that we can cut it out and truly live freely. What I have come to understand about this life here on earth is that fear will always exist. However, we have the power to conquer fear and doubt through faith and love. Perfect love drives out all fear. The Divine Spirit is perfect love, and that love lives in each of us. It is a complete love that lacks nothing. Remember, F.E.A.R. is: False. Evidence. Appearing. Real.

Action: Write positive affirmations on post-it notes and stick them anywhere you might see them. Let's tell ourselves, "I am fearless, I am capable of great things, I am powerful, I am a magnet for miracles, etc."

CUT THE CORD

Oftentimes, we don't realize we have given our power away until it's too late. I can tell you from experience that the people (whether that be a child, spouse, friend, parent, etc.) who hold your power are those who can break your spirit and your will to keep living if they were to reject or abandon you.

As I write this now, I am in deep mourning. All four of my adult children have chosen to disconnect from our relationship. In the past, this disconnect would have killed me, quite literally. Though I thought about ending my life a couple of times during this difficult separation, I came to see this as part of the process of reclaiming my power. As many of you can understand, my children were my whole world, and there was nothing I would not have done for them. I lived my life to please my children, and my only desire in life was to be the best mom I could be and to make them proud of me.

However, I made a life-changing choice that derailed our connection, at least for the time being. At this moment, I was surprised to find that the compassion and grace I had always extended to them were not offered to me in my darkest time. It was a bitter pill to swallow; one I continue to strive to understand and accept with love and gratitude. Throughout this time of estrangement, I have realized that I had given my power away to them. I could only find happiness and fulfillment in life if they were happy, and especially if they were happy with me. This is a recurring theme in my life, I have discovered. My ultimate happiness is so strongly tied to the happiness of others and, above all, to whether I am the source of that happiness. Even as I write that, I can see how vain and cringy that sounds. But it is the authentic truth. If that truth helps anyone else, I am glad to have shared it.

I had an anxious attachment style, which means I attached to people and experiences quickly, easily, and greedily. I longed to feel close to everyone that I loved, and I could not, for the life of me, understand why they did not attach as intensely to me. It wasn't until I began this self-discovery and self-love journey that I became more aware. A few years ago, when I was having a car ride conversation with Spirit (I find car ride conversations to be the most productive), I was in the throes of a pity party, feeling sorry for myself, when Spirit imparted a higher perspective on reality. The conversation went something like this: "I am tired of not receiving the same kind of love I give. I am so tired of people not being as consistent and caring about relationships as I am. I am tired of feeling like I am the only one who cares.

I thought about my dad and how he ignored and dismissed me throughout most of my life. I had longed for nothing more than to have a close relationship with my dad. I thought about how emotionally unavailable he was, and I could never connect with him in the way I had wished I could. I thought about my husband and how he ignored and dismissed me. Both men, my father and my husband, made me feel like a bother, a nuisance, and an inconvenience. I felt this from my children too. I cried from the hurt and fell deeper into my self-pity. I thought about other relationships I had with the people I loved the most and desired nothing but for them to make me feel all the love I felt for them. There must be something wrong with me. I was obviously the common denominator. Spiraling now into self-loathing, I heard Spirit ever so gently yet powerfully interrupt my spiraling with a message, one that came with images. "I wonder if you could see things from a different perspective. That you could see how you have been treated has nothing to do with you at all." It was at this moment that I saw my exhausted father lying on the couch on a Sunday afternoon, after preaching one sermon and before he would preach another one that night. I could feel his exhaustion. I could understand his burden—not just the financial burden of raising five children or the exhaustion from having to write three sermons a week to teach—but I felt the heaviness of the responsibility that he held for the very souls of his congregation. He bore their burdens, and that left little room for him to hold space for me or much else. I saw that he was trying his very best. He had tried his very best. That is when my tears began to fall—no longer tears of self-pity but tears of compassion for my father. Spirit then showed me my husband lying on the couch, resting. How his body ached after a long day of working as a diesel mechanic, how mentally and physically exhausted he was. I felt the many burdens he had from his childhood that he was still carrying. He did what he could to avoid it and numb his feelings. Because he felt so deeply. He did not have the capacity to hold space for himself, much less for me. I wept more as I realized this. I saw other people I had come to love and how they simply did not have the capacity to hold space for me, themselves, and all their work.

I understand we have all been given different levels of awareness, and our capacity to show up for ourselves while still being able to hold space for others varies. I was reminded of the times when I did not have the capacity to show up for friends and family during their difficult times. I came to believe that we are all just doing the best we can at any given moment. This realization in the car allowed me to cut the cords of judgment not only of others but of myself as well. For us to take our power back, we must cut the cords of judgment, release our burden of others' perceived inability to love us, and let go of the need and desire for such love outside of ourselves and our source. We are incredibly powerful beings created for indescribable good works; however, the things that hinder us must be cut from our lives in order to fulfill our ultimate purpose. Is it easy? No, not at all.

I first learned about spiritual cord cutting from a stranger who became a quick friend. It was December 2019, right at the beginning of my healing journey. I had recently made many major life changes. I was an empty nester. I had become vegan and started to exercise. I had just begun yoga, meditation, and journaling. I had made a commitment to myself at the beginning of 2019 that I would go and experience one new place or thing each month. What a wonderful decision that was, one I highly recommend to everyone. I learned so much about myself, and I looked forward to and enjoyed life more than ever. During this time, a friend from work invited me to a metaphysical shop in downtown Bloomington. I had never been to a metaphysical shop, as they were frowned upon in my childhood religion. I was honestly afraid of them. I was taught that I could become oppressed by demons if I ever entertained such things, so naturally I avoided them. However, since I was exploring new places and new things, I agreed to go.

When we walked into Rock, Soul, Love, we were immediately greeted by the scent of patchouli incense and a table full of colorful, beautifully polished rocks of various shapes and sizes. Naturally, the sight of rocks delighted me. I love rocks. I did not believe that rocks were energy or that they possessed any type of power to do anything that others claimed that they could. However, I was open to the experience when Carrie, a blonde-haired, bright-eyed middle-aged store attendant, asked me to pick five rocks I felt drawn to. The two coworker friends who had brought me to the shop went first with their free personalized rock reading. I eavesdropped a bit here and there, but mostly my attention was drawn to other interesting items and the fascinating claims that each item could do this or that. A candle that, if used, would guarantee fortune; bracelets with colorful beads; and claims of balancing this chakra or that chakra (I had no idea what that even was—a chakra). When it was my turn and after I had chosen my five rocks—a rose quartz, a desert rose, turquoise, an emerald, and some other stone I can't recall—she held each one over my head. She made a pile of three and a pile of two, and she said these two are not needed for you right now. I would recommend these three, though, and here's why: She began by saying, "You are a lover. I don't mean just a sexual lover. I mean you, love. You love everything and everyone. I was blown away, because yes, I felt that to my core. I am a lover. I was still very skeptical, as I was like, Yeah, aren't we all lovers? But then she shared something so specific that it would change my life. You're the mother of many children. I see that you are worried about them. I see you lying in bed at night, worried about them. Did you know that there is an energetic cord that connects you to them? No, I said. I had never heard of such a thing. When you are worried about them, you are sending them that energy. That negative energy is making them feel negatively towards you, and I see that because of this, your relationships with them are a bit strained. What? How could she have known that? She continued, Here's what I want you to do each night, she lovingly instructed. I want you to send them love and light, and then ask Archangel Michael to cut the cord between you and them. It's important that you cut the cords of others from yourself. Not only for them but for you. I understood what she was saying. But for a small moment, I wanted to resist. I didn't want to cut them away from my children. I felt that if I cut the cord between us, I would somehow lose them. However, I did not want to send them negative energy either. I didn't want them to have negative thoughts about me. I really had entangled myself so much in their energy that I did not know where they began or where I ended. I was possessive of my children, and I was obsessed with their lives as though they were my very own. My thoughts were consumed by them.

It wasn't until they had all come home to visit for Christmas later that month that I realized how pathetic my involvement in their lives had become. I awoke in the middle of the night and was convinced that one of them was cold (mind you, two of my four adult children were married and in bed with their spouses) when I found and took blankets from room to room to check to see who was cold. What the actual fuck?! Did I mention they were adults? If they were cold, I'm sure they knew where the blankets were; after all, they had lived there most of their childhood. I was literally a freak, a smother mother who not only lacked boundaries but did not understand a need for them. After all, I only had their best interests at heart. I cared; I wanted to make sure that they knew that. They knew that; I didn't need to prove that to them. What I needed to do was cut the freaking cord to say to them, I trust you to take care of yourself. I trust that if you get cold, you are self-sufficient and intelligent enough to go get a blanket and cover yourself up. I could laugh and cry at my own pathetic behavior. Just understand that if you cannot cut the cord, the cord will be severed for you. That is more painful than the latter. My enthusiasm for love and connection made me needy, and it made me want to be needed. Though I thought my intentions were pure, I quickly realized my unwillingness to cut the cord and let people be with or without me was my issue. When given no other choice, I cut the cord.

Even as I write this, I am sitting in an Airbnb, recently divorced, estranged from my children, with minimal contact with my parents and siblings, and yet I feel lighter than ever before. I have cut the cords and released them to their own paths of living, healing, and self-discovery. How they perceive me and my life path is none of my business. Do I love them? Yes, more than ever, because I love them for who they are, not for the love I could have received from them. I love them because of love, not for love. It was a journey for me to come to this realization. Our ultimate power lies in our ability to love unconditionally. And so, I will continue to strive for this supernatural power, which is love. I will search for ways to become it and embody the essence of unconditional love. This is my ultimate mission.

If I may impress on your heart one thing, it would be this: the only cord that we must never cut is the cord to the source of love. From love, all things flow and are created. From love, all things are made beautiful in their time.

A cord-cutting visualization exercise.
1. Sit or lay down in a comfortable position.
2. Close your eyes.
3. Visualize a cord stretching from you to the other person.
4. Send them love, light, gratitude, and any other positive loving thoughts that come to mind.
5. Ask Archangel Michael to come and cut the cord between you and the other person or people.
6. If possible, visualize a sword of light cutting the cord and releasing the energetic connection.
7. Do your best to place your focus on yourself and other tasks to keep your thoughts from coming back to this person (where your focus goes, your energy flows).

This chapter is appropriately entitled CUT THE CORD because many of us struggle with codependency within our relationships, and it's important that we know how to recognize the relationships that need a loving cord cutting. Trying to find the balance between interdependence and autonomy is vitally important for creating and maintaining healthy relationships. While we need each other to create a healthy family unit and a thriving society, we must also strive to be the source of our own peace and happiness.

After all, our happiness is not anyone else's responsibility. With this in mind, we must train our children and others to be their own source of peace and happiness.

CUT FOOTLOOSE

A thriving, empowered bitch knows how and when to cut loose. They have mastered the footloose and fancy-free attitude. This does not mean they are careless and reckless with their responsibilities. The attitude of a footloose and fancy-free individual is one of acceptance. She doesn't feel the need to control anyone or anything. She knows how to flow with each moment of life. She values harmony and peace. She is a confident, free spirit who remains positive in all situations and embraces adventure and spontaneity.

Making playfulness, lightheartedness, and fun one of our top self-care priorities is a must. No one likes a miserable, uptight, negative, dramatic, complaining bitch. A powerful woman knows how and when to prioritize fun, and she will prioritize it.

I love to free myself of my footwear and walk barefoot in nature, no matter what the season. When I lose my shoes and begin walking on the green grass, hard soil, mud, dry leaves, ice, sand, and the bark of the tree as I climb, I immediately feel feral. I adore this feeling of being wild and free. It seems like such a simple act—walking in nature barefoot—and yet it brings me immense joy. It is my opinion that adults overcomplicate fun and playfulness. Our fun and play are typically planned and feel within the realm of our control. We don't usually like surprises, and our inability to be flexible with our fun time is tested if things do not go according to the itinerary. Have you ever planned a vacation that did not go according to plan? I'm sure we have all experienced the disappointment of a vacation gone horribly wrong.

I had flown to a close family friend's wedding in Palm Beach. The weather and wedding were beautiful. It was a long weekend getaway for me, just a few weeks before my divorce was final. I had a wonderful flight to Palm Beach and a delightful few days. Naturally, I did not anticipate any complications with the flight home. It was Sunday morning, and I had a total of 6 hours of travel before arriving back home. We made it to Atlanta Airport, and as we were preparing to land, the plane was rerouted. Our plane landed at a small airport nearby, along with two additional large commercial aircraft. We were told we would be back in the air shortly and just sit tight. Three hours later, while still sitting on the tarmac, things got heated, and I don't just mean the stagnant air. The shitters were full, the beverages and snacks were all gone, and the once patient and understanding people were starting to get agitated. Finally, the pilot gave us instructions to deplane. We walked into the small airport, full of passengers. People were talking and telling perfect strangers about where they were going and what they would be missing if they did not get to their destination on time. Honestly, some of their stories tugged at my heartstrings. One stands out to me: a young family with two small children trying to take a European cruise that was leaving the next day. It would be the last vacation that they took with the young mother's terminally ill father. The whole family was going to be together on the cruise. She told me that her sisters' families and her mother and father had already arrived at the planned destination to take the cruise the following day. I watched as she kept her composure and continued to care for and play with her children while her husband desperately tried to make other arrangements to get them to their destination. We were told we would be flying back to Atlanta soon, two more times within a 6-hour period of being inside the airport. At the sixth hour, we were given hotel room vouchers for the night.

Throughout this experience, I observed how people on my flight were handling the many disappointments and setbacks, and I was so proud of us humans. People were making the best of a shitty situation. I heard laughter as strangers exchanged jokes and stories. I watched the children play and interact with their parents. The mood was overall peaceful and positive.

Even the next morning, as they delayed our flights an additional half a day, people were making the best of it by bonding over our mutual situation, looking out for each other, and creating friendships. I cannot say the same for the flight that arrived just after us. They were angry, cursing and shouting at the airport workers, us, and each other. People from my flight and I shook our heads and laughed as we commented and agreed, saying, "What good does it do to get upset? Just make the best of it. If we find ourselves stuck in a less-than-ideal situation, it's important to make the best of it. Find the silver lining, make it a plot twist, and create an opportunity for an unexpectedly excellent adventure. This is the attitude a winning bitch has. Life is always happening "for" her and with her, not to her. She sees positive outcomes in every challenging situation. She doesn't fight the current of life; she accepts the moment for what it is and continues to flow freely.

Footloose is one of my favorite movies—the 80's version, not the remake. The music was epic, the dancing was stellar, and the message was, for me, relatable. Growing up as a Pentecostal, the preacher's daughter was anything but footloose and fancy-free. In fact, no dancing, no going to dances, and absolutely no secular music was a real experience for me. If it had not been for my mother, who did not grow up in this religious organization, I doubt I would have had the privilege of attending any dances at all. Our movies and television shows were closely monitored. We had a strict Saturday night curfew of 10:00 p.m. We were required to be in attendance every time the church doors were open. This meant Sunday morning, Sunday school and worship service, Sunday evening, Wednesday night fellowship, and weeklong revivals. As teenagers, we were not allowed to miss attending church, not even for work, especially not for work. Church and religion were our way of life. If it sounds extreme and oppressive, you would be correct in your assumptions. Being that my personality was so agreeable and accommodating, I never really considered an alternative way of life or that a happy, thriving "heathen" lifestyle was even possible.

Without bashing too much on organized religion, I find in my quest for truth and awareness that much of my life was shaped by fear, and most of that fear was conditioned in me by the religious institutions I grew up in. I am not suggesting that this is the case for everyone. I understand that different people are motivated by different things. Some are most influenced by love, others by fear, and a few have a healthy balance of both. My personal perception of my upbringing was that I was motivated most by fear. It could be because that was the most dominant tool of manipulation used to control myself and my siblings. "If you do this, this bad thing will happen to you. If you do that, the wages of sin are death." Don't even think XYZ or you will be back slidden and left behind to take the mark of the beast and go to hell or have your head chopped off. No, that is not a joke. I love my parents. I believe my parents intentions, like all good parents' intentions, were pure. I have no doubt that their motives came from a place of love and concern. I believe they believed all the teachings that they were taught. I witnessed how they walked the walk. My parents are good Christian people. I would have considered myself a good girl, a rule-follower, and a people-pleaser. I did as I was told with little to no pushback. I never missed church, I did not drink or party, and I did not smoke or do drugs. I dressed modestly, I did not listen to the devil's music (Rock n Roll), and I tried really hard not to fornicate. I really did. Looking back on my teen years, in all honesty, the most freedom I felt was when I was naked under a blanket in the back of my boyfriend's pickup truck, parked in the middle of the Arizona desert under the starry night sky. There is something so pure and innocent about being young and in love for the first time—and naked, don't you think?

I have found that much of connecting with the free spirit, which I believe exists in all of us, is about connecting to the natural innocence we inherited at birth. Sex is natural. Having a sexual drive is natural. And one of the most pleasurable ways to play is through physical touch, through the exploration of our bodies, and through the body of the one we love or love to enjoy. I'm not exactly sure when physical pleasure became a taboo subject that causes most of us humans, especially within the religious community, to recoil in disgust. But here we are, evolved humans still acting like middle school children during sex education with awkward discomfort. I imagine many of you are feeling a bit squeamish at this very moment. Nevertheless, it would be irresponsible of me to write about empowerment through play, fun, and freedom without discussing one of my favorite playful activities. As mature adults, there are few socially acceptable things that grown-ups can do without looking immature and a bit weird (although I will still do many childish things anyway) when it comes to expressing our playful nature. Sex, however, is a perfectly acceptable form of adult play, and if you are doing it right and with the right partner, it is, or should be, incredibly fun. Health experts agree the benefits of a healthy sexual life include lower blood pressure, better heart health, an improved immune system, better quality sleep, immediate natural pain relief, increased libido, improved self-esteem, a decrease in depression and anxiety, increased intimacy, and human connection, just to name a few. The benefits of having sex go beyond physical pleasure, mental satisfaction, and emotional bonding; sex is a spiritual experience. The best sex is transcendent; it is sexual pleasure that leads to a higher state of enlightenment and an energetic frequency of heavenly bliss. Sex is a powerful universal force that merges our spirit (divine self) with our body (earth). This is the act of bringing heaven to earth. Heaven is your divine self, and earth is your physical body. In this regard, sex becomes a sacred spiritual activity. Many have called sex a religious experience. Call it what you will; I will continue to call it FUN. It is my very passionate opinion that sex is one of the best things about being a spirit and having this human experience. Our sexuality is a powerful force, and a woman who fully embraces her sensuality with natural curiosity and unbridled confidence is an empowered woman who will enjoy ruling in and out of the bedroom.

Since we can't live every moment of our lives in the bedroom and we still want to make life as fun as possible, as often as possible, and since we need to eat, let's have an experience of it. Food can be fun. If you are a foodie, and I believe many of us are, you'll agree that trying new restaurants' drinks and food can be a fun and entertaining experience. This is another way for us adults to enjoy a fun activity together. Whether with family, friends, or a romantic partner, we all find joy in making memories that center around one of our other favorite pastimes, food. Here's my suggestion: if you want to add more spice to your life, forgo the chain restaurant for a locally owned and operated restaurant. Some of my favorite restaurants are farm-to-table restaurants, where a local restaurant grows or purchases fresh produce, as well as buying their dairy products and meat from surrounding farms. Many of our holidays and other social events involve and often revolve around food. My family was no exception. As my adult children got older, I tried to come up with activities that would keep them engaged and off their phones so that we could all spend time together. I bought a table-length Teppanyaki Grill, cut meats and vegetables of various kinds, a variety of sauces, and a couple options for rice one holiday, and it was a success. Each of them experimented with and created their own favorite dish. They talked to each other and helped each other, and oh, how I enjoyed hearing the sound of their laughter. Let's be honest, as parents, our children's laughter is one of the best sounds on earth. I enjoyed watching and listening to them interact with each other, and at the center of the activity was "food."

Another fun way to cut loose is to crank up the music and dance. Nothing puts a human in a joyful state quite like music and shaking your booty. I ran an in-home daycare for many years, and if I noticed the children were getting bored and starting to fight, I would proclaim a kitchen dance party. It often happened when I was preparing lunch, so it was usually held in the kitchen. I would turn on some upbeat fun music, usually a CD of my daughter's (who's a singer-songwriter), and we would dance, sing, and twirl around. There were no more tears, and it put an immediate end to the tantrums and fighting. I think that if adults, when we were in a conflict with each other, decided to turn on some upbeat music and dance together, it would have the same effect on us as it does on children. I believe laughter would ensue, and most of what we were upset about would diminish. I know it works for me every time. If my heart is feeling heavy and I want to feel an immediate lightness, I crank up the tunes and dance my little heart out. Music and dance are not just free therapy. It's an outlet that provides a fun way to move your body (exercise) and connect with and uplift your soul.

My love for nature began in the back seat of a packed station wagon, where I watched the canyons of Utah fade away into the Arizona Desert, too young to fully appreciate how magnificent the wild was. We spent most of our vacations in the great outdoors, camping, hiking, and sightseeing. That's what poor people did back in the day when they wanted to take a vacation. In this respect, I am thankful I grew up poor. I used to envy my friends who spent their summer vacations at Disneyland. Until I was an adult, I went to Disneyland. No thank you. I much prefer seeing natural wonders, such as the Grand Canyon. However, I do prefer to have a bed, toilet, and shower. Growing up, we had a tent. One of my favorite trips was to Yellowstone National Park. We watched the bison graze along the side of the road so close that I was sure if I stretched my hand far enough, I could touch them. We visited Old Faithful, which was faithful, and swam in hot springs near our campsite. We didn't have much money, but looking back now, I am so grateful for those moments we all shared together in that olive green station wagon. Like most children, I looked forward to summer vacation and taking a trip. It was a much-needed break from the usual routine.

A few years ago, when I began this self-discovery and self-creation journey, I questioned why we live this way. Human conditioning? I understand that most of us aren't even aware that we spend much of our lives waiting—waiting for the trip, waiting for love, waiting for a pregnancy, waiting to finish school, waiting. So, it makes sense that most of us live our lives just waiting for our next planned vacation. Having a get-away on the calendar makes life feel more bearable. It helps us tolerate our jobs and even find gratitude for the work that we do. We dream of a life we don't need a vacation from, of having the freedom to move about when and how we please, focusing on the hobbies and activities that make us feel alive.

It was this realization that inspired my awareness of this "waiting to enjoy life." I was waiting until I was off work to enjoy my day, waiting until the weekend to live my best life, and I started finding and integrating ways to create the day of my dreams. By intentionally or spontaneously integrating more fun activities, as previously mentioned, we can stop waiting for the planned vacation to enjoy our lives and start enjoying our lives today. When we look for opportunities to incorporate more meaningful and inspired fun ways to play in our everyday lives, life becomes more enriching and fulfilling.

Living a footloose and fancy-free lifestyle doesn't have to cost much. Don't let social media posts convince you that you must have a high-priced, exotic vacation and spend a lot of money to enjoy life. The footloose and fancy-free lifestyle is a mindset that says no matter where I am or what I am doing, I am going to make the best of it. I am going to find extraordinary joy in the everyday little things. It's having a playful attitude and a lightness to your soul. Being in touch with your natural childlike state, wild and free.

Consider and make a list of 12 things you haven't done and places you haven't been. Start small. For example, that little restaurant or coffee shop you've always wanted to try. Then pick a day, put it on your calendar, and go have that experience. Put at least one new adventure from your list on the calendar each month. Being intentional about having new experiences makes your life feel more alive. It's time for everybody to cut footloose.

1.
2.
3.
4.
5.
6.
7.
8.
9.
10.
11.
12.

THE FIRST CUT IS THE DEEPEST

Female friendships are a bitch! The bitches we choose to ride or die with are going to impact the trajectory of our lives. Female friendships will make or break us. It is of utmost importance that we choose wisely. You know the saying, "Bad company corrupts good morals." I define bad company as a false friend, one who you cannot trust, who is a constant complainer, who gossips, who is never happy, who is full of drama, and who is a bundle of negative energy. Now, I understand we all go through shit, and we have times in our lives when we are struggling, so I'm not suggesting we cut a friendship off during these times. Being a fair-weather friend is just as toxic and something a "bad company" friend would do. We don't do that. Let's define what I believe "good morals" are. To me, good morals are positive energy, love, joy, peace, trust, patience, kindness, generosity, etc. You feel me. All the good, easy-flowing vibes. How do we attract these kinds of good-energy friends? We become this kind of good energy friend. It all begins with us. A great place to start is by evaluating and learning the lessons from our failing platonic female relationships. We compare them with our healthy, thriving connections. This is a good way to gauge how we want to feel or not feel in relationships. Our feelings are important; they act as a sort of antenna. As we tune into and trust our own gut instinct, especially when choosing friends, we can avoid a lot of heartache down the road. Once we become intentional about the type of friend we want to be and the quality of the friendships we would like to create, we are more likely to achieve this goal. I call it a goal because our connections and relationships with the same gendered individuals are crucial to our growth and development. Who we choose to surround ourselves with can mean the difference between success and failure in all areas of our lives. Be intentional when selecting your inner circle.

As for me personally, I am a girl's girl. I love females, in a strictly platonic way. I love female energy. I grew up with three sisters and gave birth to three daughters. I have been fortunate to have had the most positive and uplifting relationships with females. With that being said, I have experienced my fair share of female wounding. I have spoken in depth with many of my friends about the deep scars that have remained from female friends and family members. It really made an impression on me that each friend I spoke with was able to recall, in painful detail, the first memory of what I would refer to as "the sister wound." No matter what age this wound occurred, it has had a lasting impact and, in some ways, has shaped our present friendships, what behaviors we can tolerate, and what behaviors are our friendship deal breakers. Why is the first cut the deepest? Because it is our first experience where the bonds of trust have been severed. Our childhood innocence and the illusion of unity and harmony with those most like us have been forever altered. The lines have now been drawn in the sand, and the all-inclusive playground group play becomes "You can't play with us."

When I pondered my own first cut, my "sister wound," it took me all the way back to kindergarten. This was the first incident I could recall where I felt the sting of betrayal from a friend. Though her name escapes me, I remember she was my best friend. She was the girl I always tried to sit by during circle time, stood by in line, and played with at recess. I remember feeling that good feeling of mutual friendship. The feeling that proclaims, "I have a best friend." We attended a small Christian private school together. Every day, we ate our lunch in the classroom on the circle rug. Each of us brought a lunch that had been packed for us at home. As I unwrapped a sandwich from the parchment paper, I was immediately disappointed. There were two slices of stale wheat bread (which I hated; I much prefer Wonder Bread) with a fatty piece of shredded roast beef from our dinner some nights before and a small bit of mustard smeared on one slice of the bread. I leaned in and whispered in my friend's ear, "My sandwich looks like poop" (not shit). I didn't know that word back then. She looked at me with big eyes, sighed with disgust, got up, walked to where the teacher was sitting, and whispered in the teacher's ear. The teacher got up from her chair, went to her desk, and wrote a note. She called me to come to her; she handed me the note and told me to take it to the principal's office. I still remember the layout of the principal's office. I stood frightened in front of his large desk as he read the note. He talked to me and explained to me that saying poop was a bad word, and because I had said the word, I would be punished. I was then told to pull down my panties. He then bent my tiny little body over his knee, pulled up my skirt, and I watched my platinum blonde pigtail sway as he paddled me vigorously on my bare back side. I did not feel remorse or shame, as was the purpose, I imagine. I felt four new feelings that I could not name at the time, but I can clearly articulate now: betrayal, injustice, humiliation, and blind rage. With tears and a look of defiance, I pulled up my panties over my stinging bottom, pulled up my skirt, and vowed to never speak to that girl again. I do not recall if I ever spoke to her again or not. But I never forgot that first experience of betrayal, as it was painful in more than one way. I wonder if you remember your own first friendship wound—that cut from a friend.

We moved a lot during my childhood, so most of my friendships were brief and unremarkable. I made friends easily and enjoyed many wonderful friendships while they lasted. I learned at a young age how to detach when it was time to move on, cutting friendships off with ease. Although I have been fortunate to have the same few best friends for over 30 years, sadly, none of my childhood friends made it to this chapter of my life. However, the few best bitches I have are the truest, and trust me, THE BEST bitches ever!

"Friendship is so weird. You just pick a human you've met and you're like, "Yup, I like this one," and you just do stuff with them." My oldest best friend tells this story about how we became friends. It's a story that I love so much that I must share it. I had just moved to a small midwestern town with my then husband and three young daughters. We moved into a house next door to a beautiful single mother of three children around my children's age. Right away, I felt like I had won the neighborhood lottery. Our children became fast friends, and our personal properties became shared properties, and it was wonderful. The children would play together as we watched. Kim was still healing from a recent divorce and new to the area, and I had just moved from Arizona and did not know a soul. I liked her, and I wanted to be her friend. However, I could sense that she was resisting our friendship, and I don't know what possessed me, but I said to her with great conviction, "You know we are going to be friends." She tells people, in jest, that she had no choice in the matter, and from that moment on, she accepted the friendship. We have been through a lot together, and when I needed a place to retreat after I separated from my husband, the shelter of her home and friendship were the first places I knew I needed to be. I cherish our friendship, and I am so grateful for her compassion and unconditional love. She is one of the wisest humans I know. I have learned to value having a friend who is wise and imparts that wisdom to me. If we want to be wise, we must choose wise friends.

"A friend is one that knows you as you are, understands where you have been, accepts what you have become, and still allows you to grow." There is a beautiful woman in my small hometown. Beautiful face, figure, and soul. There's something about Mary, and everyone can't help but love her! I was no exception. From the moment I met her, I was charmed. We did not become instant friends. I met her, and it wasn't until some years later that we became the best of friends. If I'm being honest, I think I feel like I won her friendship by default. You see, she was going through a nasty divorce, and her now-ex-husband was out to destroy her. He had turned just about everyone in our small town against her. To make matters worse, he turned their church family against her; they attended a large church in the nearby big city. Her best friends turned on her, our community began to shun her, and it was heartbreaking to watch. I don't recall exactly how we started talking, but we did, and we became the best of friends. I defended her good name and reminded people that she was a person of good quality and character. Mary has done the same for me over the years and even now. She has my back, and I have hers. I will never forget one particular phone call and visit with her. When Mary was going through chemotherapy and her beautiful hair was falling out, she called and asked me to shave her head. She came over to my house, and there in my bathroom, I did all I could to maintain my composure as I took the razor to her remaining long locks. She was smiling and kind, as she always is, as she thanked me and hugged me goodbye at the door. When she left, I lost it, and I cried for the rest of the evening. I was so afraid of this horrible disease, cancer. Watching several of my dear friends battle this disease has made me appreciate my friendships more than ever. My Mary has long hair now, and we are still the best of friends.

Few experiences are as painful as having to cut off a best friend. The death of a friendship can be devastating, even though it is necessary. In my recent past, I confided in a close friend a secret that I needed to get off my chest. She betrayed my confidence by exposing my secret. After she gained my trust, I felt safe sharing with her about my past and sharing some of my past errors in judgment and the things I had learned. When I found out that she exposed me, I felt betrayed and humiliated. I still love this woman very much, but our relationship will never be the same. The trust was broken, and though we may continue to stay in contact professionally, the probability of re-establishing a close friendship is highly unlikely. Still, I choose to focus on the good that came out of the situation. This secret, this truth, set me even more free. I now understand that just because you love someone enough to trust them does not mean they love you and can be trusted. I have learned to respect my boundaries and the boundaries of others, and I have learned to have grace, for often we do not know what we do or the consequences that we will inevitably all face. Trust is the foundation on which all friendships are based, and all other values build upon this foundation. A friend who cannot be trusted is not your friend. As I sit here and reflect upon my friendships, I realize how incredibly fortunate I have been to have had the incredible female friendships I have had. That made me think about the kind of friends I attract and the kind of friend I have been, and I felt both humbled and grateful that my female friendships have been so blessed.

"If you have good friends, no matter how much life is sucking, they can make you laugh." It's Jess. While I was going through my divorce, a friendship bond strengthened between my friend Jess and me. We have a lot in common. We are both chatterboxes, love rollercoasters, 80's music, and exercise in the great outdoors. She is as childlike as I am, and we can just be, have fun, and act goofy together. When we are going through a difficult time, we need friends like Jess who want to help us take our minds off our troubles. After I signed my divorce papers, she drove us over two hours to Six Flags for some rollercoaster fun. I cried a lot for many months prior to the divorce. The truth is, I still cry some days. But having that break during my season of grief was like coming up for air while I felt like I was drowning. It's important to have friends that take us out for coffee, tacos, and fun while we are suffering. To have friends that put a smile on our face, a song in our soul, and a giggle in our belly is priceless.

"True friends aren't the ones who make your problems disappear. They are the ones who won't disappear when you're facing problems." Debbie is sweeter than any snack cake and one of the best. I met Debbie when I was hired by my former employer. While she was giving me the new employee orientation, I remember looking at her and thinking to myself, "We are going to be the best of friends. I like her." I was not wrong. We did become the best of friends. We spent every lunch hour together. Whether we were eating shitboxes (Chick fil a chicken nugget, waffle fries, mac n cheese, buffalo wing sauce, and ranch sauce), shopping, or going to the gym, we were work besties. While I was separating from my husband, her husband was being transferred to Virginia. I never imagined moving to Virginia. I wanted a fresh start, and Debbie and her husband invited me to come and stay with them as long as I needed until I found a place. I gratefully accepted their gracious offer. Because of her generosity, I was able to have the fresh start and new beginning that my soul longed for. I will forever be grateful to her.

These are just a few of my favorite friends. The woman who has impacted my life the most, especially recently, "A friend loves at all times." I am grateful that these women have remained my besties through thick and thin.

Over the years, I have learned there are beautiful females in our lives who will love us fiercely, celebrate our wins, comfort us when we cry, and lift us up when we are feeling weak. The women who remind us of our strength and value—these are our soul sisters. The family we chose. Letting go of the deep wounds from the females who did not match our essence and who did not value our friendship is a sacred act. It requires a deep level of compassion and forgiveness. It requires understanding and patience. It requires us to stand in our own power and say, "No matter how I was treated in the past or how I may be treated in the future, I know who I am, and I can trust my ability to move past the pain of any betrayal, rejection, and disappointment into a gracious place of acceptance." Finally, it requires us to remain open and embrace the positive female relationships we are building. To focus on the women in our lives who have been our greatest inspiration and source of divine love.

"There is nothing on this earth more to be prized than true friendship." Thomas Aquinas

Action:

List five qualities you have that make you a true friend.

1.
2.
3.
4.
5.

List five qualities you want in a true friend.

1.
2.
3.
4.
5.

List five things that are important for you to experience in your friendships.

1.
2.
3.
4.
5.

CUT THE CRAP

All personal transformations begin with one very powerful decision. The decision to cut the crap. We have all reached that breaking point and know when change needs to happen. However, we cannot change what we do not acknowledge. We cannot create something or someone new if we do not accept who we are right now and look back at how we got here. Taking our power back from people, places, and things requires radical acceptance.

We cannot change our poor spending habits if we do not take an honest examination of why we spend beyond our means. We would love to say, "I'll just stop spending. I'll go on a strict budget and get myself out of debt." Most of us cannot just do that by sheer will alone. We must dig deeper and ask ourselves more honest questions. Such as, Why am I overspending? Why am I using retail therapy as real therapy? Why does buying something new make me feel so good? And then so bad later?

We cannot change our physical weight and health if we do not ask ourselves the deeper question of why we turn to food for comfort. Why do we eat when we're bored? Why is food a reward? What is the root cause of my addiction to food? When we become aware of the root cause of our emotional attachment to anything, such as food, we can begin to build a healthy relationship with that subject.

This kind of honest reflection is what I mean when I say "Cut the Crap." We must do this in order to become self-empowered; we must find out who, where, and what holds power over us.

We cannot change our relationships if we do not start with our own unhealthy patterns and behaviors. For me, some of the questions I have been asking myself look like this: Why do I feel so anxious and upset when the people I love are angry or having a bad day? Why do I feel the need to fix them? Why do other people's negative emotions have such a strong negative effect on me? These are the real-cut-the-crap questions I dug deep to ask myself: What questions do you need to ask yourself?

After reflecting on these questions, I noticed my relationships have struggled for many years, and I've come to realize this is because I am incredibly uncomfortable with negative emotions, either from myself or others. A better question would be, Why do I care so much about other people's feelings? Who died and made me the emotion police? Why do their emotions affect my mood so much? Why am I giving my power away to others and their negative emotions? As I ponder these questions, I am slowly and carefully getting to the root of the issue. When I reflect on this question in relation to my own personal transformation, I cannot help but remember my last phone conversation with my mother. How upset I was, I was crying about my divorce and the strain it has put on my relationship with our children. I was explaining to her how abandoned I felt by my family, and when I finished pouring my heart out to her, she asked if we could change the subject and talk about something more pleasant. That immediately triggered childhood memories of arguments my family would have—how my mother would lose her shit, whenever we would have a passionate disagreement or even a calm debate or disagreement. She would shout over everyone and say, "I just want peace." I remember a couple of times, on our way home from church, us children would get into an argument. My mom would wait until we got to a stop, then jump out of the car and slam the door. My dad would have to roll down the window and drive slowly, begging her to get back in the car. Her reactions were always very effective, as we spent the rest of the car ride home in terrified silence. I would eventually break the ice by making everyone laugh or saying something nice and positive. I wanted to fix the anger and the uncomfortable silence. I wanted to give my mother what she wanted, "peace," but at what price? Let me be clear: I am not blaming my mother, who did the best she could raising five children.

I realize now that I continued that "peace at all costs" into my own family dynamic. I ended up marrying someone who triggered this trait of my mother in me. I became someone who wanted to keep the peace and keep conflict at bay, no matter the cost. My husband would become angry and punch holes in walls, clear the counter of every dish, stomp and slam doors, shout, and curse. His method was effective; I fell into old, familiar patterns of staying quiet until the storm passed, then fixing it with sex or sweeping everything under the rug with a cheerful, calm energy. I made sure to keep the children as busy, happy, and engaged as I could. I would never receive an apology, and I never demanded one either. I held it together by making excuses, taking the blame, and telling myself things would get better. If I can just be better, be less, be more, and be the best wife and mom, I can do that by making sure I catch every negative emotion from everyone else in the family and calm it down before it escalates. I was hypervigilant, and now I realize I was probably not much fun. I was exhausted. After a night of physical, mental, and/or emotional abuse, I would get up the next morning and pour out half the vodka and refill it with water. I just wanted "peace."

Here is where I must take full responsibility for my role in this situation. I refused to see the situation for what it was. Why? I wanted to believe I had a happy home life. I had only wanted to have a happy family, and my inner being was shouting, I JUST WANT PEACE, but false peace comes at a price. You see, I was, to my knowledge, very good at hiding the truth of my situation, even from my children, or even from myself, for that matter. I'm not sure they had any idea of the abuse I was experiencing. I put on a brave face for them and for me. Queen of compartmentalizing. Later, when speaking to my ex-husband, pre divorce. I told him all that he had put me through, and he explained why and what was happening inside himself that made him drink too much, withdraw into himself, his depression, and the excuses for being neglectful and abusive. I understood. But what truly stood out to me in that conversation was him saying I should not have protected him or the children from what was happening in the home and that that was on me. He was right; I should have fought back. I should have called the police; I should have allowed our children to see him taken away in handcuffs. I should have divorced him and had my children grow up in two different home environments. At least that would have been the truth—the reality. But instead, I chose to deceive myself and others. Radical acceptance. The consequences of that deception would be life-altering and devastating.

If you want to become the most empowered version of yourself, you must peel away every layer of falsehood until you find the ugliest, most brutal truth. The truth about what we've done and who we have become will set us free. Once we are free from the burden of pretending to be someone or something we are not, we become unstoppable. There beneath that ugly truth are endless possibilities for a solid foundation where we are to build a new and improved version of ourselves. What do they look like, sound like, and move like? Close your eyes and imagine how you would feel if you were living, moving, and being in your personal power. If people, places, and events could not take you out of your own personal frame (energetic frequency).

We all long to break free from the need for external satisfaction and, even more so, to break free from external disruptions. To take our power back, we need to be free from the things that anger us or make us feel something we don't want to feel. For example, (this is one used often) you are driving along singing one of your favorite songs on the radio, and you're happy and feeling great when someone cuts you off and you must slam on your breaks. If that driver causes you to lose the moment of happiness that causes you to grumble or curse them for cutting you off, is your mood and behavior the fault of the driver?

Cutting the crap requires taking full responsibility for every aspect of our lives. No excuses, no victimization, no spiritual bypassing, and no toxic positivity.

My challenge to you is to begin to observe and write down situations or people who alter your mood and behaviors based on their actions. Journaling about these situations daily can help us become aware of our areas of weakness. When we are aware of those areas, we can take positive action towards reclaiming our personal power. Take an honest inventory of the situations that cause you to feel like you are not being true to yourself. These are the people and situations who are here to teach us, grow our awareness of ourselves and the power we possess, and create and maintain our own peace. True peace in any situation or circumstance. To proclaim "all is well. Life is happening for me, not to me. I have the power to control my emotions and my moods. I am responsible for myself and the life I am creating. I am a powerful being.

CUT ABOVE THE REST

You are the best and only you that has ever lived! Each of us was created for a unique purpose, which is all our own. There has never been and there will never be another set of fingerprints exactly like yours. The fact that you even exist is a miracle. Considering we were created and exist for the purpose of the world needing someone like us, this should make us feel extraordinarily powerful. I believe once we realize the power of being the real, unfiltered, and authentic version of ourselves, the best years of our lives unfold in the most miraculous ways. One of the best things about aging is how comfortable we feel in our own skin. Our skin is weathered by the years; we don't have that glow of our youth, but simply put, we don't give a shit. Most women, by the time they reach midlife, know their worth. Therefore, no outside opinions of us can shake us. Freeing ourselves from other people's expectations and limitations is key to stepping into the most authentic, powerful version of ourselves. When we recognize our own value and discover that we are, in fact, priceless and irreplaceable, we will stop giving people discounts. We will stop saying yes when we want to say no. We will value our time, money, and talents.

I was recently listening to several relationship coaches on TikTok give their opinions on what makes a woman or man a "high-value" woman or man. While I agree with most of what they were saying, I was still a little troubled. In my opinion, all of us are of high value. We were created that way. So, what makes a high-value person move into a version of their higher self? The only actual difference between a regular bitch and those we perceive to be high-value beings is that high-value beings know their worth. They have confidence in their individual worthiness, and because of this, they know they deserve the best. Why not? Don't we all deserve our definition of the very best? In my opinion, what makes something of high value is based on how rare something or someone is. I would argue we are all rare because each of us is wonderfully and uniquely made. We were not born to be cookie-cutter copies of anyone. We are all one-of-a-kind. Our set of fingerprints is a powerful reminder that we are the only ones and a magnificent reminder that the Divine Spirit is limitless in creation. There is no limit to what can be created when we step into the most authentic version of ourselves with gratitude, grace, and confidence. Do you want to be a high-value baddie? The first step is remembering and believing that YOU ARE ONE.

I get it; it's easier said than done. So, here are some helpful steps I took and how I remembered who I was created to be: How I lovingly removed all the past limiting beliefs and a lifetime of conditioning to become the most authentic and empowered version of myself. Take or add what works best for you; again, we are not one size fits all types of people.

1. Have a vision for the life you want to create. Who you want to be, and what you want to do
2. Take inventory of your past. Think of your childhood and what you were naturally drawn to (history matters).
3. Make small changes and adjust daily.
4. Experiment with your life.
5. Daily affirmations and an "I am journal"

Want to be a cut above the rest—the best version of yourself?

1. HAVE A VISION

"The man (human) who has no vision will undertake no great enterprise."
-Woodrow Wilson

Who do we want to be? How do we want to act? How do we want to feel? What are our beliefs? These are just a few questions I asked myself while I was creating each higher version of myself. Notice I said versions (plural) because elevating growth occurs in phases. There will be many versions of ourselves as we progress on our self-healing, self-improvement, and self-empowerment journeys. Think of yourself as a house. Creating your best self is like building a house. It happens in phases; it's often frightening at the beginning, messy in the middle, and takes more time and investment than we had originally anticipated. But when every detail of your dream house comes together and everything is even better than you imagined it could be, the outcome, the reward, will far outweigh the cost of the pain you had to endure to embody your new home, your new self.

When I first heard of vision boards, I thought they were a bit silly. However, I could see the value in having a vision for the life I wanted to create and the type of woman I wanted to become. I began to write it out. I began to speak it out. I began to visualize the person I wanted to become. I'll be honest, I did not read more than two or three self-improvement books; instead, I wanted to rely on my own intuition and internal guidance system. I wanted to learn by trial and error. In essence, I wanted to write the book. That is the vision for my life right now. To complete this book, I want to share my experiences to encourage others to live a free and empowering life. However, the vision did not begin here, and it does not stop with the creation of this book. The vision of the creation of my life is ever-expanding. I once had a vision of having a large social media presence. When I reached a collective (between TikTok and Instagram) of almost 200,000 followers and had a couple of videos go viral, I felt I had achieved this envisioned goal. I love to envision things now, and oftentimes the things I have a vision for manifest. I had a vision to be a children's book author and publish my children's stories since I was 24 years old; I am 52 now. I published my first children's book three years ago, at 48 years old, and I recently published my third. Each of these books began with a vision. I could see and envision the illustrations. I could feel how it felt to hold one of my books, tangible, in my hands. I imagined reading them at schools and libraries and someday to my grandchildren. My vision became a reality. Yes, I had to do the work and put in the effort, but it was fun because this is what I wanted to do.

When a sewing client would bring me what I felt was a near impossible article of clothing to create a memory bear with, I would lay in bed at night and create it first in my mind. I had a vision for how I would cut and construct the item to make it a successful product. That vision was often executed even better than I had hoped. I believe it is in our nature to visualize the outcomes of our lives, whether negative or positive. And I believe we possess within us the power to achieve the unique visions that have been given to us. Our mind is a powerful tool we can use to build the life of our dreams. Have a vision not only for the big goals but also for the outcome of everyday experiences. I guarantee you that it will astound you. All you can accomplish in your life if you allow yourself to envision a positive outcome.

Before my divorce was final, I had planned to move to Virginia. I imagined living in a two-bedroom, two-bathroom condo with a view of the ocean. I envisioned living a block or two from the beach. I saw myself walking on the sand in the water, listening to the waves, and smelling the fresh ocean air. It was as though I was already there. I imagined a tree park or nature path near my condo where I could enjoy my time amongst the trees. I love trees. In my vision, I had paid no more than X amount of money. I was able to purchase this envisioned place because I imagined selling our family home for more than anticipated. This vision is now my reality. Of course, this was not the life I had envisioned prior to my divorce. I had a different vision for that life. That's the thing about having a vision. You must be willing to be flexible and allow yourself the space to create different possibilities for different versions of yourself. Don't be rigid with your vision, or you will become frustrated and disappointed. Work with where you are and what you must do to make the best possible version of where you are now. I assure you that you will get where you want to be if you stay positive, flexible, and creative with your vision.

I have a future vision for this book, a podcast, and public speaking. I see it, hear it, smell it, taste it, and touch it as though it were already mine. Our thoughts are creating our vision now. What are your thoughts? What is your vision for today, tomorrow, and beyond? It's already yours, and you deserve it.

2. TAKE INVENTORY OF YOUR CHILDHOOD INTERESTS

If you are anything like I was, I didn't have a clue what my purpose or vision was beyond being a mother and wife. I was content to live the rest of my life blissfully, unaware of my wants and potential. My basic human needs were met, and that seemed good enough. I had completely forgotten about my passion to publish a book, and my sewing machine was in a box tucked away in the corner of some closet in my home. My life and my world revolved around taking care of my family. By the time I became an empty nester, I was empty. I had no direction on what to do next. One night, while lying in bed, I wondered who I was as an individual. Not just as a mom or wife. What do I enjoy doing? What kind of woman do I want to be now? A thought from the Divine Spirit entered my mind. What did you enjoy pretending to be as a child? This may hold the key to who you are and what brings you joy. I thought about it for a moment, and all of these childhood memories came flooding back to me, along with things family members had said I was a natural at. I remembered how I loved to play, pretend, and create. I liked to write stories and plays and act them out. I would be standing in the middle of the concrete cinder block basement, where the acoustics were just right, and I would sing or make up a dramatic monologue. Later, I would come to discover that my mother would often stand at the top of the stairs and enjoy my performances. I used my imagination to create stories, commercials, and soap operas and act them out. My siblings often remarked that I was an entertainer; my grandfather called me a character, and my mother would tell me I had the gift of gab. I imagined I was many things, from a teacher to a flight attendant, a Dallas Cowboy cheerleader to the princess of Egypt. That's where my creative and sometimes wild imagination and my love for entertainment and storytelling came from. By going back to the beginning, when I was so full of the magic of life and life was so full of wonderful possibilities, I was able to connect with myself again. You see, I believe that before we arrived here as limitless spirits in tiny human bodies, we were given a one-of-a-kind, unique personality, passion, and purpose. We were sent to earth to learn, heal, grow, and remember. I believe that the younger we are, the more we remember, and the unremembering happens as we age, until we can't remember why we came here at all. Our responsibilities and pressures in our daily lives—just trying to survive—empty us of memory. This is why I highly recommend returning to your childhood and the things you were most drawn to. See how these things align with who you are now. Could this be the key to unlocking the memory? It was for me.

3. MAKE SMALL CHANGES AND ADJUSTMENTS DAILY

I am 5 feet, 2 inches tall. I have always been a tiny girl/woman. While going through the "change" of life, I put on fifty plus additional pounds. The weight gain came so slowly that I hardly noticed it was happening. I went up several pants and top sizes; however, when I looked in the mirror, I didn't see the weight gain. Delusional, I know. I adjusted the type of clothing I was wearing, choosing to wear loose fitting tops and stretchy pants. If I was wearing jeans, I would wear a waist shaper. I didn't really let my weight gain affect my life. I still thought I looked fine. I figured if I had an event or summer was around the corner, I would just starve myself for a few days, drop 10 pounds in a week, and then I'd be good (that's what I used to do, successfully). That no longer worked. You see, I wasn't conscious or aware of my body, my diet, my mindset, or my life. I was on autopilot. I never really took the time to imagine that I could be anything different or better. I believe this is why I let my health decline. That all changed the day I saw a photo of myself and my son. I looked... I'm just going to say it FAT. I was bloated, and I looked unhealthy. I remember hiking the sand dunes in Michigan that day and feeling uncomfortable and out of shape. I struggled to keep up with the others. I love to hike; I love the outdoors, and I was not accepting this for myself. I made a dramatic change to my diet shortly after that. I began exercising and taking better care of my body and, as a byproduct, my physical appearance in general. When I look back at pictures from that time, I barely recognize myself.

This moment of self-awareness began my transformational journey. It took me 18 months to lose those fifty pounds. During those 18 months, I began to take an inventory of my life, the areas I needed to heal, my daily habits, and my mindset. I set daily doable goals, congratulated myself enthusiastically at the end of the day when I met my goals, and embraced myself with compassion when I fell short. With every little goal I met, I began to grow more confident and self-assured. I believe this is why I was successful in reaching my larger goals. I had a vision for the woman I wanted to be today. I did not look so far into the future version of myself that I became attached. I just wanted to enjoy the creation of myself without the pressure of arriving at any certain destination. My daily vision was to feel healthy in mind, body, and spirit a little more each day. It was to do the things I promised myself I would do that day. I became conscious and aware of all my daily decisions, knowing that all these choices matter. Each day, I give myself the space to expand my vision to a new level and show up as her. My personal advice, and perhaps an uncommon opinion amongst the self-improvement community, would be this: do not hold tightly to a certain version and outcome of who your distant future self will be. For example, in my vision as my highest self, I see myself on a large stage, standing in the spotlight with a full audience in attendance. But you see, I am not attached to this vision. I have other visions as well, which I hold loosely. If they come to fruition, that is wonderful. If they do not, that is wonderful as well. By allowing yourself to build a better "me" gradually, with gratitude for each day's victories, we will be amazed at how fun and addictive creating this envisioned self actually is. It won't feel like work at all. It will feel like play, because it is.

4. EXPERIMENT WITH YOUR LIFE

Be your biggest fan and loudest cheerleader. Do it for yourself so you can be a cut above the rest. Get excited! Be enthusiastic! But whatever you do, do not beat yourself up when you fall short. There will be moments every day when we feel like we have fallen short of our goals. On these days, filling ourselves with kindness, compassion, and grace is a must. Be patient as you navigate this new personal exploration. Allowing ourselves to see it as a fun experiment makes it a fun experience.

In 2019, I made a sort of new year's resolution. I decided I wanted to broaden my interests and try new places and experiences. I set a goal to try something new each month. It could be a new restaurant or activity. I might drive to a new destination I had never been to and explore the town or hiking trails. But I did it; each month I adventured to a new place and enjoyed a new and exciting experience. I hiked new trails, rescued a kitten from the shelter (I had never had a cat), tried new restaurants, drove several hours for a day trip to see Lake

Michigan, went to a metaphysical shop, drove to Chicago to meet a favorite author, attended a banquet and had her book signed, became a vegan, attended a yoga class, etc. This year was the beginning of my own personal journey into the self-discovery that would lead to empowerment. More on this in the final chapter. That year changed me, and I became a bit obsessed with trying new things. It encouraged me to take ballet, belly dancing, pole dancing, rock climbing, and bouldering. I pushed myself way out of my comfort zone, but damn did I have so much fun.

Experimenting with life is one of the most enriching actions we can take. We tend to lose our childlike wonder. We begin to accept life as it appears, and we forget that we still have many fun things to learn and experience. We forget that we are here to live and to collect as many wonderful memories of experiences as possible. The pressures of life and work remove us from our inner child, our inner being, and we forget to play and appreciate the newness of life. There are many things we have never tried. I encourage you to go ahead and live a little, starting now with one new adventure a month. It doesn't even have to be expensive. Don't just wait for your next planned vacation to start enjoying your existence here on this amazing place called Earth. Experimenting with life regularly will expand your world in the most marvelous way and make you the most interesting human. You will fall in love with your life again; this will empower you and make you the best version of yourself that you can be.

5. DAILY AFFIRMATIONS AND AN "I AM" JOURNAL

I have discovered after years of suppression that I do, in fact, love words. Go figure. I especially love positive, affirming words. I have always loved giving them, and I love receiving them as well. Growing up in a home where I love you's were never said, and positive reinforcement through words was seen as flattery, which was a sin. Encouraging words were few and far between. I learned to live without words of affirmation. Which was a good thing because my now ex-husband was not a word-of-affirmation person either. I did, however, receive plenty of verbal criticism and abuse. As you can imagine, that affected my self-esteem, leaving me empty and feeling unworthy. As I began to heal my traumas, I sought a way to reverse the damage that had been done to my self-esteem through verbal abuse and emotional neglect. It occurred to me that the only way to correct the negative impact was to collect and deposit more positive words. That was when I had the idea for my "I am" journal. (Side note: I discovered they made an I am" journal; I missed my opportunity to cash in on that one.) I firmly believe that the words that follow "I am" have the power to create our reality. Who we believe we are has everything to do with how we show up in the world and what we receive from it. "I am" is one of the most important words we speak to ourselves. Choose wisely.

I wrote in the back of the journal all the things the creator of the Divine Spirit said that I am and that we all are. When we are born into this world, this is who the Sacred Spirit says we are. Say it with me,
I AM......
Loved
A child of the creator
Chosen
Holy
Blameless
Forgiven
Predestined
Alive
Seated in heavenly places
A masterpiece

Cherished
A promise
Bold and confident
Delightful
Citizen of Heaven
Peace
Powerful
Protected
Complete
Beloved
A conduit of love and light
A friend
Justified and redeemed.
Free of sin and death
Heir of Creation
Accepted
A saint
A sacred temple
Triumphant
New creation
Righteousness
One
Blessed
I AM LOVE

I then began to fill it with things that people would say to me in real life or on social media. For example, if someone at work said, "Thank you, You have been very helpful," I would write in the journal. I am appreciated, and I am helpful. People would tell me I was beautiful, and I would write, I am beautiful. Every kind or even seemingly kind thing that was said to me I wrote in my journal with the I am in front of it. I wrote positive quotes and the definitions of the positive words as well. I filled the pages with self-love. I cannot begin to tell you how these positive affirmations that I was filling the pages of my journal with helped heal me and fill my soul. I bought affirmation cards for work and shared them with my coworker friends too. I had affirmations on post-it notes on my desk, at home, and stuck to the items in my purse. The power of our words is undeniable. They can heal or hurt. I don't need to write in my "I am" journal anymore, and I don't need to fill myself up constantly with affirmations, because they work.

I can vouch for the fact that affirmations work if you work. If you are willing to make the effort to recognize, read, write, and recite these positive mantras, you will fill your mind and soul with life affirming energy that will aid in creating the most empowered version of yourself. No matter where you are on your journey, just remember that you are a cut above the rest. You are the best at being yourself, and because of this, you are worthy of all the goodness and love that this life has to offer. The fact that the creator of the Divine Spirit decided the world needed one of you makes you a cut above the rest. BIG BITCH LOVE from me to you!

CUTOFF SHORTS

Life is too short to worry about the size of our thighs. So, bitch, wear the shorts. Don't just wear shorts; rock the hell out of them. I am thankful that we live in a time in our society when all body types are being embraced. Plus-sized models, entertainers, and influencers are showing up and speaking out about body positivity. All body types are welcome and celebrated. Crop tops and cut-off jeans are for all ages and body types, and society at large is not just simply accepting this; we are enthusiastically embracing it with love. I am hoping this is a sign of our evolution as humans and that body shaming is a thing of the past. Ancient history. So, let's cut the negative self-talk in keeping with the times. Because we are beautiful, our bodies are divine.

Personally, I have experienced body shaming on both sides of the spectrum. I have been shamed for being fat and shamed for being too thin. There were two defining moments that created a distorted image of my body in my head. These moments reinforced what I already understood with regards to the standards of beauty—how most people judge the value of a person based on their outward appearance.

I had never felt particularly pretty. In fact, I had been told by my best friend's mother that I was not at all pretty but that I was cute (she said with pity). I was not the most beautiful, cool girl in school. That was my oldest sister's role. She was the family art piece. The one my father proudly presented to congregations whenever we went for a church interview. Being cheerful, friendly, and outgoing, I was "the personality," and it was my job to warm up the crowd. Be the opening act, so to speak. Because I did not have a shy bone in my body, and my beautiful sister did, this was just the natural order of things. When one is not pretty, you are often told that you have a great personality. I was told that often. I now wonder how many times it was due to the fact that they pitied the ugly duckling. Having the most beautiful sister in town was both a blessing and a curse. She was perfect, and everyone would comment on the perfection of her hair, complexion, hourglass figure, puppy dog eyes, etc. Every girl I knew wanted to be her, and every guy I knew wanted to date her. I admired my sister's beauty and felt mostly lucky to be her little sister. I would study her. The way she put on her makeup, how she styled her hair, and how she dressed so that I could one day look like that too. To say that I idolized my sister would be an understatement. So, imagine how much impact the things that she would say had on me.

She was like most older siblings; she enjoyed picking on her younger sister. I remember her and I sitting in the back seat of the car on our way to Sunday evening church when she looked over at me and said, "You know you're going to be the fat one in the family." Side note: My sister is one of my best friends, and I fully understand that we were children and children say stupid things they don't really mean. With that being said, at that moment, as a 12-year-old girl, I felt crushed. The hot, unwelcome tears that I tried desperately to hold inside were burning as they streamed down my cheeks quicker than I could catch them and wipe them away. I could not retaliate because I believed she was right. I could never compare to her beauty, and the truth was, I was a chunky little girl, and I always have been. I would be lying in the bathtub, cursing my belly rolls. I would lean into them and grab hold of them with my hands, believing that if I could have a flat stomach like the other girls, I could be pretty too. At that moment, I promised myself that I would never be the fat one in the family. For most of my life, I kept that promise to myself, sometimes to the detriment of my own health. From that moment on, my top priority was to be thin. This promise led to the second defining moment with regards to my personal experience dealing with negative comments about my body.

Around the same time the following year, a boy in eighth grade commented, "You're so flat, the walls get jealous." This comment was made to me almost 40 years ago. 40 years, and I still remember it like it was yesterday. That joke has impacted the way I see my breasts to this very day. Haha, I jest, but there is some truth to this. Our words are so powerful, especially when they are spoken to our bodies. The words of others will affect how we view ourselves for many years to come. This is a reminder to make those words beautiful and empowering.

I managed to return to a healthy average weight after I gave birth to each of my four children. It wasn't until I hit mid-life and became premenopausal that I packed on the pounds. I had changed careers, going from running a daycare in my home and working in a busy salon where I was on my feet most of the time to a desk job. My once-active body was now sitting all day long. In four years at this office job, I had gained almost fifty pounds and was physically feeling awful. I decided I needed to get my health under control. I thought about how I did not want to burden my children with health issues that I could have managed with diet and exercise. I took full responsibility for my body. I became vegan and began working out three to four times a day at a local gym. The weight was coming off slowly, and one evening, when I was feeling particularly disappointed with my progress, I looked in the mirror at my reflection. I scowled. I wanted to scold the reflection of my body in the mirror for eating that small brownie early in the day, but something changed. I softened my gaze and smiled at her instead. I moved closer to the mirror, looked into my own eyes, and smiled softly. I said to my body, "If I love you just the way you are right now, could you love me back?" Tears began to fall as I suddenly had a new appreciation for my body. Immediately, memories that had been stored by my body began to flood my mind. Memories of my body carrying and birthing my children. I thought, "This body is a miracle-making machine." I thought about sex and the pleasure the body can give and receive. "I am a Divine Spiritdess,"

I thought. I looked at my skin cancer scars and chickenpox scars from childhood and said, "I'm a survivor." I noticed my eyes and my hair. I looked down at my feet to see how these feet and legs carry my body safely everywhere I go. The hands that help, heal, and hold. Our bodies are fucking amazing! They deserve so much love for everything they have carried us through. All the hurt and healing, all the trials and triumphs—our bodies have been a constant support. It was so strange how, from that moment on, I saw my body as its own separate part of me. Worthy of much honor and respect. From that moment on, I loved my body fiercely, and together we lost those fifty pounds and have managed to keep it off for three years now. I ran a few 5K's, which I never imagined being able to achieve, and I have enjoyed feeling more comfortable with fewer aches and pains.

No matter our weight or body type, we should love our bodies fiercely and treat them well. These bodies are the only ones we will have, so I think we should care for them the best we can. By eating as healthy as possible and making time to move, we can create a healthy body. Which creates a happier, more fulfilling life. A complete and fully empowered woman honors and respects her body and treats it like the temple it is. No matter the size or shape, she is confident in her body and wears cutoff shorts or whatever else she wants. She understands that the one-size-fits-all mentality does not fit her. She feels empowered, not insecure, by the uniqueness of the shape of her body. She embraces the changes her body goes through with loving acceptance and grace.

I'm often shamed for wearing the clothing I enjoy wearing. As a woman in my early fifties, I still love to rock a crop top and a tiny bikini. Hell, I would go naked if I could. My body image has done a complete 180. I've always had this body—not in this particular shape, of course—but I haven't always had this mindset. The old me would have hidden her thigh dimples and stomach cellulite. The past version of me would have covered her rolls and sagging skin. This version of me is not ashamed of her figure or her aging body. The way I see it, if people don't want to see it, they don't have to look. Respectfully. I've spent too many days feeling self-conscious. With age comes a delightful freedom. But why wait until we are older to enjoy our beautiful bodies? I often look back at pictures from when I was in my 30s and wish I was that fat again. Haha I can't believe that at that time I thought I was fat. I was perfectly beautiful. We waste so much precious time belittling our cute little figures in our younger years, only to regret not appreciating them more then. No matter where you are on your body image journey, I hope that by reading this chapter, you will see your body in a new, beautiful light. We are fearfully and wonderfully made. Our bodies are a miracle in motion. Take the picture. No matter what you weigh, what you are wearing, what your hair looks like, or if you have makeup on or not, If someone you love wants to take a picture of you, let them. Sadly, one year when I was at my highest weight and lowest point in life, my children tried to take pictures with me, and I did not want to be photographed because of the way I looked and felt. I didn't want to be seen. One of my daughters creates a photo book each year with her favorite moments and people. That year, I was missing from the book. Not one single photo of me made it into the book. So please swallow your pride, love your body no matter what, and take the damn pictures. You'll never regret the pictures you took, but, trust me, you will regret the pictures you didn't take. Because those moments will never come again.

Our body image affects many areas of our lives because it impacts the way we see our desirability. It is hard to be confident when we are unhappy with our outside appearance. Even if we are confident in knowing we are wonderful humans on the inside, we all long to be seen as just as beautiful on the outside. When I realized I had packed on the pounds and that I did not see the lustful gaze in my husband's eyes towards me anymore, it changed the way I moved in the bedroom. I had always been a very sexual person. I had an overall healthy view of my appearance. I felt that I was desirable according to society's standards (youthful, firm, and thin). Then it seemed as if, overnight, I had become this saggy old maid. I felt frumpy and dumpy, the farthest thing from a sensual Divine Spirit. I dressed in oversized, baggy clothing. The kind that makes people ask, "When's your due date?" I hid my body from him and the world as much as I could. When it was bedtime, I avoided intimacy by telling him I would be in bed soon. I would wait to hear his loud snoring before quietly slipping into bed. The times we were intimate, I just wished for it to be over as quickly as possible. It was hard for me to concentrate on feeling the moment of pleasure when I was noticing all the fat rolls on my body.

My sexual desire was directly correlated with my body image. I know a lot of you might relate. When I love my body, I feel energetic and magnetic. When I feel great about my body, my sexual energy is off the charts. I love sex. To me, it is as important to life as food and water. That's why maintaining my positive body image is of the utmost importance to me. Now, no matter what age or what size my body is, I will be celebrated as a sexually sensual being.

It takes mental work and effort to love your body through all its transitions. Body-image affirmations are incredibly helpful. Here are a few of my favorites to use: Affirmations rewire our brains and change our thought patterns from negative to positive. I have found them to be the most effective tool in reframing my thoughts and helping me love my body for all that it is.

My body is a sacred temple that houses divine spirits within.
My body gives me pleasure and is a pleasure house for others to share.
My body is sensual.
I feel at home in my body, and I appreciate it.
Images of my body bring me joy.
My body is worthy of respect.

I respect my body by feeding it loving thoughts.
My body is a miracle.
My body is perfect for me.
My body is wonderfully made.
I feel confident in my body.
I love the way my body feels.
I honor all the things my body can do naturally.
My body amazes me.
My body is always listening to me, so I tell my body how marvelous we are.
My body is a part of my team, and I celebrate our existence with enthusiasm.
My body is unique, so I never compare it to anyone else.
My body is not a work in progress; my body is a complete masterpiece in motion.
My body supports me and keeps me going even when I don't make the best choices for us. I take care of my body, and my body takes care of me.

Add some of your own unique personalized body positive affirmations to this list:

CUT FROM THE SAME CLOTH

We are all cut from the same cloth, and the same threads of love are woven throughout the fabric of our lives. Collectively, we are one. A complete, beautiful tapestry, created by the source for all good works.

I am a third-generation professional seamstress. I grew up with the comforting hum of the sewing machine. Both my grandmother and mother helped contribute to the household income by using their natural sewing talents to help people who lacked them. So, when the Spirit inspired me with the name of this chapter (by speaking it to my heart), I got excited. My initial reaction was, "Now why didn't I think of that?" Then the Spirit so lovingly reminded me that together we create good works.

Have you ever experienced sharing wisdom or insight with a friend, only to have them call you a few months later to tell you the exact same thing? She is so excited to claim her new treasured knowledge. Enter my ego; on the tip of my tongue, I began to say, "Bitch, I'm 100%

sure you are just regurgitating what I already told you. Don't act like you are teaching me something I haven't already taught you." Enter Spirit, who immediately intervened with a powerful reminder: "There is no such thing as an original good thought, word, or deed that did not first originate with me." There can be nothing new under this sun without me. All good things come from love, the source of love. When Spirit drops the mic, you zip it. Trust me, it's that powerful.

We are all connected to the same source of energy and have unlimited access to the never-ending wisdom of the divine. Being that we are all connected, we are all one with the creator, and we are all individuals connected to each other in that oneness. When we really consider this mystery, we can more easily view others as part of ourselves. "That which you see in me is that which is in you." This is a quote by Maitrey Miranda that I find powerful and often refer to as a great reminder of our connection to one another. I love Rumi's version even more: "The beauty you see in me is a reflection of you." What a wonderful reminder to overlook others faults in search of their beauty. Because it will be that same beauty that we will discover within ourselves. Now, we are appreciating them while also appreciating ourselves. When we find fault in others, we are subconsciously finding the same fault and our own shortcomings.

Another thing I have learned firsthand when it comes to the spirit is that things are not always as they appear. Therefore, it is always best to keep an open mind.

I used to be very rigid in my spiritual beliefs and faith practices. As I mentioned before, I grew up in an organized religion, so I was like most good Christians. I believed in the theory that angels existed and that there is a spirit world somewhere out beyond our reach that we must accept on faith alone. Any attempt to contact or connect to my guardian angel or anything in the spirit world was wicked. Until I have had multiple experiences, which I cannot describe as anything other than supernatural, I wish to establish the fact that I am not, as they say, "Woo Woo." I prefer to ground my reality in science and things I can hear, see, taste, touch, and smell. I preferred to let the spirit world exist, and I will just be here accepting that. But that is not the reality of the experiences I've had.

It all began when I was driving to work one spring morning as the sun was rising and the sky looked like it was on fire. I was in awe and could not wait to pull over and take a picture of the sky. Yes, I am one of those people who gets excited about the sky. As I was driving, I was conversing with the Divine Spirit, as I often did, and I was telling the Spirit that I wanted to experience them in a bigger way. I felt that the Divine Spirit that I knew in church just felt so small and untouchable. I wanted to experience the miracle of connecting to him the way Moses did when he went up to the mountain and asked the Divine Spirit to reveal his true glory. I wanted to have this kind of connection. I told them that I felt they were so much more than I had experienced, and I wanted more, so much more greatness. I wanted the bigness and the glory of the Spirit. Be careful what you wish for.

As I mentioned before, I am a professional seamstress. I make a modest income creating memory bears, animals, and pillows. I create these items from people's deceased loved ones' clothing.

The first time it happened, I wasn't sure if I was imagining the contact. While working on two bears for a widow and her newborn baby, her husband came through. I could see him in a vision just letting me know he was observing, and he thought this was so cool. He gave me a message to pass along to his wife. Even though I did not know him in real life, I felt as though I knew him. His personality, I mean. I was a bit unsettled, and I did not wish to deliver the message. I did not want to be perceived as a weirdo. However, I felt a powerful pressure that would not relent. I cried, and I agreed to give her the message if I saw her. I planned not to see her. This was during COVID, so the likelihood of me seeing her felt as though it would work out in my favor. I pulled up to their house, got out of the car with the two bears, and there she was walking down the long driveway to meet me. F*ck! The pressure was building as I handed her the bears. I took a deep breath and began by saying, "Please don't think I'm weird. But would you be open to hearing about the experience I had while working on the bears? I believe your husband has a message for you." She was so happy to hear it and confirmed the message. I got in my car, and the pressure that had been upon me lifted immediately as I heard a "thank you." I was exhausted after that. I went back to my house to take a bath and slept for hours. I still couldn't believe this had happened, and honestly, I was totally okay if it never happened again.

I began to doubt and thought I had imagined the whole thing. Until it happened again, and this time it was so detailed and unmistakably direct, I could no longer doubt that this supernatural thing was actually happening through me. I had just cut out a necktie to put on a bear. The clothing belonged to an older gentleman who had passed, and I thought the bear needed a tie. His daughter had found me on Facebook and mailed me two button-up shirts so that I could make her and her mother each a bear. That was all I knew about the client and the deceased. As I began to sew the necktie, I heard a stern man speak to me (a stern thought in my head that is not me): "I did not like neckties. I wore bolo ties." This was such a specific and demanding request that it froze me in my tracks. I said, "Okay." I did not argue with the voice in my head. Haha. I spent some time trying to decide if I should reach out to his daughter and ask her about this experience. I did not make the necktie, and I finished that bear and began on the next. It was a white button-up shirt with some silver embellishment. As I was creating that bear, again the man spoke to me, "I want this bear to have angel wings." I had never made angel wings before. However, I thought, "Yes, that is a brilliant idea." I cut out angel wings and completed the bears. I finally gained the courage to reach out to my client. I sent her a message, "I hope you don't think this is weird," and I explained the experience I had with her deceased father. I waited hours to hear back. During this time, all I can think is that she thinks I am coo-coo for cocoa puffs. However, she replies with a few photos. One photo was a picture of her father wearing a bolo tie and a few bolo ties from his collection. She confirmed he worked for Sears and had to wear neckties, and he hated wearing neckties; he only wore bolo ties. The other photo was a picture of her cabinet and tattoo. She said the angel bear was mine. I collect angels and angel wings, and I have a tattoo of angel wings.

The year after COVID was, sadly, a very busy year for me. Not only was I working with clients who had a loved one pass on from COVID, but I had many clients who had a loved one pass on from suicide. Now that I think about it, it makes sense. Many people were suffering mentally during the pandemic.

One client, in particular, will forever live in my heart. She had come to the side door of my 130-year-old farm house, a tiny woman with a heap of finely pressed shirts still on their hangers. Though she greeted me with a smile, I could see that sorrow weighed heavily on her spirit. She was very thin, and her eyes were sparkling beneath the hollow of the eye sockets. I felt an immediate connection to her, as if I knew her, though I had never met her before. I quickly invited her in, offering to take the shirts from her. She declined and sat on the couch with a stack of shirts in her lap. Suddenly, I felt her son there with us. This had never happened before. So quickly and abruptly. "That's my mom! Give her a hug for me. Tell her I love her." I spoke inwardly to him and said, Please leave, not now. He listened and left. At that point, I did not know how he had passed. She told me that he was 33 and told me how handsome and full of life he was (which I already had experienced). She showed me pictures of him. And he was very handsome indeed. She, much like the others who have lost a loved one to suicide, spoke softly, as though ashamed, and explained how he had taken his own life. I could feel her pain; her suffering was evident. I told her that sometimes their loved ones will come through to communicate with me (I never mention this upfront, as I do not want them to be disappointed if they do not come through). But I knew he was eager to communicate. Her eyes lit up, and she said, "Yes. Oh, I would love that."

Over the course of the next couple of months, while creating a dozen or so bears from her son's shirts, he was with me often. I gave her a message from him and one to his fiancé and her daughter as well. The messages were detailed, confirmed, and greatly appreciated. However, it was the message he gave me to give to his father that really gave me some understanding of the impact this type of work has on my clients. You see, I was not asked to make a bear for his father. She said he could share hers. I think she thought he would not want or appreciate a bear. But her son insisted, and he told me not to deliver a message to his father verbally but to write down what he was going to tell me and give it to him. He gave me a very detailed message, and I could feel the depth of every word. I had to pause often to wipe tears from my eyes so I could see what I was writing. The one thing about connecting to those on the other side is connecting to this boundless heavenly love. How this pure, powerful love feels when experienced here on earth. It's intense and overwhelming. I gave his mom the bear and the letter, explaining to her what her son had requested. A few days later, I received a text message from her. She told me she had not seen him cry since the funeral but that he sat on the end of the bed, held the bear, read the letter, and wept. The last time I saw them, the dad, who had been mostly MIA during my bear drop-offs, was full of curiosity as he asked me many questions about my work. He confirmed the details of the letter and thanked me for listening to his son's insistence that I make this extra bear (I refused to charge for it) and for the letter.

I had come to believe that it was only when working with the clothing of the deceased or a sewing client that I had this ability. But soon I would become aware of the fact that I was able to connect random (or not so random) people to their loved ones. A friend of his mom, through his aunt, gave me her name and told me she passed before his mother. They were coming through together, and for reference, there is no possible way I could have known her name.

Recently, I made a young bartender cry on the job in Gulf Shores, Alabama, when I gave him some guidance and connected him to his biological father, whom he had never met and had just passed a few months prior. He did not tell me this. He confirmed this information after I asked. I don't know how I know what I know. I have just come to trust and accept the information that has been given to me by the Divine Spirit. What I do know is that there are many confused, hurting, angry, and sad people in the world who need to hear a message that there is light and life beyond this existence. I am delighted to be a conduit for such light.

I have a beautiful collection of personal experiences and stories like these that remind me of the miracle of life, our connection to a divine source, and our connection to each other even beyond the grave. We are all cut from the glorious hem of the garment of the source of light, cords that cannot be broken. Whether in this lifetime or the next, we are woven together by threads of love for eternity. I belong to you, and you belong to me, and we all belong to the great creator, Spirit. We are each uniquely individual, yet we are one.

I am not special. This spiritual gift, the discernment of spirits, is available to us all. I believe we all have unlimited access to each of the gifts of the spirit. In fact, as you read further into my book, you may question what makes me good enough and qualified enough in the Spirit realm to have such divine access. And the answer is this: Nothing. I am nothing without the spirit of the Divine. As the apostle Paul wrote, "I do not understand what I do. What I want to do, I do not do, but what I hate, I do. And I do what I do not want to do." This is what it means to be human. So, once, when I was feeling unworthy of these divine experiences, I inquired of the Spirit, "Why me?" and I laughed because Spirit did not skip a beat. "This isn't about you," they said. Haha, I love that response. The divine spirit can take a flawed ordinary woman like me to deliver messages to people who have been divinely placed on the same path. Wouldn't it be so cool if we were all just walking around giving each other divine loving messages all day long? Heavenly.

There is a phenomenon I am confident we can all relate to. An occurrence that I believe we would all agree is too miraculous to be a coincidence. Have you ever been thinking about someone, maybe even someone you have not thought about or heard from in years, and as you are thinking of them, you receive a message or a phone call from them? This is not a coincidence; this is a connection. Two people share a moment on the same universal energetic frequency. I have had this happen to me many times.

One time stands out in my mind. I did not know this individual very well, but I felt a deep connection to them when we first met. So, our contact was sporadic, and I rarely reached out to them first as they were always very busy. But one night I was working on my bear's in my sewing room, and out of nowhere I felt intense panic and fear. I started to gasp for air, and I began weeping uncontrollably. It took a moment for me to bring my awareness back to myself. This was not my energy; I was tapping into someone else (which I've been known to do, and it can be a bit frightening). I asked who it might be, and I received my answer. I fought the urge to reach out to them. I did not reach out to them that night. I thought the feelings from this contact might pass, but after a sleepless night, I woke up, got ready, and went to run errands. While I was sitting in the bank drive-through, my angel came to me and said you must message them now. I pulled into the bank parking lot and wrote, "Are you okay?" They replied, "No. My mother was rushed to the hospital, and it is not looking good." A couple of years later, this same friend would save my life not once but twice with the same question, "Are you okay?" At just the right time. Please trust me, when you are feeling that strong urge to reach out to someone, do not think it is a random coincidence; you might be the instrument Spirit uses to help, heal, or even save someone's life.

In reading this chapter, I hope you can see how powerful your presence on this earth is and how each of us matters to each other. Our connection to the Spirit and to each other is the meaning of life.
Take a moment to reflect and perhaps journal about a time when you connected with someone or had a spiritual moment. Notice how life is a miracle, and nothing happens randomly.

SHORTCUTS

Most shortcuts are bullshit! How would you feel about driving across a bridge designed by an engineering company whose motto was, "We make 'em cheap and quick." No one wants their infrastructure designed and built cheaply and quickly. So why are we convincing ourselves of this idea of building ourselves cheaply and quickly? Why are we always looking to cut corners in search of shortcuts with health and fitness, spiritual growth, financial security, relationship rescues, etc.? If Rome wasn't built in a day, why do we put so much pressure on ourselves to build the life of our dreams overnight? In fact, most of us dream of getting rich quick, being lucky in love, and becoming an overnight success story. We play the lottery in hopes of a quick, easy fix. We purchase the latest fad diet supplements guaranteed to help us lose inches without changing our diet or exercising. We listen to podcasts and purchase books on healing and growth because knowledge is power, but we do not apply the knowledge we gain. We create content for social media in the hopes that we'll go viral and overnight become an influencer. The fact of the matter is that our culture glorifies overnight success. Sometimes for doing nothing of great importance. I should know. One evening, I posted a 5-second reel to my Instagram page. It had a voiceover message about women in their fifties looking younger than ever. I was wearing a leather fringe vest (no top, but not revealing too much either) and a flowy floral dress that was made to look like a skirt. I was sitting on a log, smiling playfully. In one week, that five-second reel received over 5.5 million views, and my account grew over 100,000 followers, reaching over 6 million accounts. In the Instagram world, that is considered an overnight success. I realize that many of my friends on Instagram would be overjoyed by becoming a seemingly overnight success and boosting their following so quickly. Initially, I was shocked and then very grateful, but the fear quickly set in. What if I'm a one-hit wonder? What if all these people who follow me don't enjoy the rest of my content? What if I can't keep this going? Something I had always hoped to experience had happened, but now what? What I can tell you about my experience is that nothing really changed except for the fear and anxiety that were revealed in my soul. I had more growth work to do. I understand that healing and growth are not linear, and the work is never fully complete.

But I say, Bitch, don't cut your power cord. We have access to the divine creator of divine spirits, and we are powerful co-creators when we stay plugged in. We take our power back when we take personal accountability over everything in our life experiences. We even have the power to rewrite the "negative" stories we've told ourselves for years. We can transform our perspective from one of victimhood to one of victory if we are willing to see things from a higher point of view. If we can develop a mindset that sees the positive in any negative situation, we will succeed in finding fulfillment in life. I've worked hard to build my personal life around feeling good. Feeling safe in my being. Feeling love over fear. Feeling in alignment with my calling. Whenever I am feeling stuck in fear or negative thoughts, I have an internal guidance system that reminds me what to do. How did I develop an understanding of this internal guidance system? Over time. It has taken a great deal of time and even more discomfort to practice what I preach. Here is one of my favorite life hacks for working through and transmuting negative thoughts and emotions.

1. Recognize the negative thought, feeling, or emotion.
2. Name the emotion, thought, or feeling.
3. Sit with these feelings for some time.
4. Take three deep breaths (keep your focus on each breath) while saying, "I am safe."
5. Keep your thoughts in the present moment.
a. Listen to the sounds around you.

b. Feel the textures of a surface near you or the clothing you are wearing.

c. Look at the objects around you. Focus on things you enjoy seeing.

d. Focus on a scent near or around you. Light a candle or incense.

6. Release the emotion, thought, or feeling and replace it with a positive thought or affirmation.

The most important thing to remember about bringing ourselves back into alignment with the naturally powerful being that we are is staying in the present moment. Our personal power exists only in the present moment.

Self-improvement takes a great deal of self-discipline. As we can see, it is not a quick fix. However, it is worth the effort; it takes some time to effectively work through our negative thoughts, feelings, and emotions. The great news is that each time we experience the same uncomfortable feeling, we become better at recognizing and quicker at releasing the experience from our minds, and with practice and overtime, it will cease to bother us at all. Of course, there are quick fixes and shortcuts to feeling better for a moment. These quick fixes provide only temporary relief and often involve unhealthy substances, which can lead to unhealthy addictions. Alcohol, comfort food, retail therapy, hookups, and excessive porn viewing are quick and easy ways to relieve stress and pressure. A fast way to increase dopamine and give us a temporary high. However, if we are searching for permanent peace and lasting joy, we are going to have to take the scenic route. A route that will require us to walk through both our shadows and light. Developing our internal guidance system, aka intuition, is the key to long-term success in all areas of our lives.

Bitch cut the dead-end dieting out. There are no shortcuts for health and fitness. There is no magic pill, no miracle wrap, and no pound-shrinking drink that will give you firm abs and a 25-inch waist. If you want to get fit and healthy, it takes a major mindset shift, knowledge of your body type, and the best nutritional program for you. It is going to take a lot of work. While I was going through pre-menopause, I gained weight. I gained 50 or more pounds, and I was the heaviest I had ever been. I had tried every diet during these five or so years. I could not seem to keep the weight off; in fact, as you can probably guess, I gained more weight with every failed diet. In my desperate attempts to lose weight, I deprived myself of proper nutrition. I'd starve, I'd binge eat, and I'd spend a ridiculous amount of money on diet and nutritional supplements. I tried it all. I even tried those crazy IT Works wraps. In fact, I believed in the results from the wraps so much that I joined the program as an affiliate. I drank the greens, took the pills, and used the wraps. It didn't take long for me to realize none of these things could deliver the results I was investing in. Eventually, I dumped the program and tried another program, the carb cycle diet, and then the military brat diet. Nothing I did gave me the body or health that I was after. The only thing that was shrinking was my bank account. Eventually, I discovered the secret. Do you want to know the secret? You're not going to like it. Sacrifice and hard work.

1. No sugary drinks; at least 62 ounces of water a day.
2. No processed sugar, more fruits and vegetables.
3. As little processed food as possible for more all-natural foods.
4. No more, and I mean absolutely no more fast food. A good rule of thumb is that the more your food looks like the food it's supposed to represent, the better it is for your health.

5. Move your body for at least 30 minutes a day. I would recommend an hour for better results.

I took my diet to a whole other level and became vegan. I was a hard-core vegan for 3 years. Let me tell you, it was the best thing I have ever done for my overall health. After one week, I had more energy than I could remember. I felt great! And it was that great feeling, that energy, that kept me going to the gym almost every day and taking PiYo classes a couple days a week. It took me 18 months to lose 50 pounds, but the best part was the way my body felt. My mental health had improved exponentially, and I was loving life again. With all that extra energy, I was able to create a thriving small business and challenge myself with new hobbies. There are no shortcuts to the life of your dreams, and that includes fitness and health. It's hard work and sacrifice, but the rewards far outweigh the sacrifice. If you really want to change your life, stop making excuses and start making room for this next healthier, happier version of yourself. I am confident that if someone like me can do it, so can you.

Bitch, don't cut your money tree. If the goal is to get our bag, become independent, and become wealthy, then we have our work cut out for us. There's that word again, "work." Add to that the sacrifice it takes to get out of debt, pay your house off, and retire before you're 65 years old. I am not going to pretend I have done all those things, but I do have friends who have. I am currently debt-free; even my car is paid off. I was able to purchase my condo as well because my ex-husband and I had a home we owned and lived in for almost two decades, so we had plenty of equity in our home. With that being said, I have not even come close to reaching the financial freedom I am longing for.

However, I have a few close friends and family members who have worked hard and made wise money moves so that they can enjoy their early retirements. One friend in particular, who is in her 40s, just paid off their over 20-acre property and beautiful home in the country. They are completely debt-free and love life; they will be able to retire in their fifties and enjoy freedom from debt and work. It sounds like a dream come true. When I asked my amazing friend how they were able to accomplish something this extraordinary, especially in this day and age, she wasn't smiling, and she always smiles. She got very serious as she told me how hard they worked and all that they sacrificed to achieve their goal. No family vacations, no new cars, no eating out (family of 5), etc. They were intentional with their money, well organized, and stuck to their strict budget. "That must have sucked," I thought. She admitted it did at the time. But I talked to her just after she made her very last mortgage payment at 46 years old, and she never sounded happier, freer, or more excited. She had already booked a few trips to visit family members and have some much-deserved fun. I feel as though I should tell you that these are not wealthy people. They are a middle-class family; she is a teacher and coach, and he works for a large insurance agency. By societal standards, they are just your average family. With a plan, hard work, and sacrifice, we can improve our financial situation whenever we are ready.

Here are 10 practical ways to improve our financial situation now:
1. Create a budget.
2. Track your spending.
3. Look for ways to cut unnecessary spending.

4. Review all your insurance policies regularly to see if you can get a better deal elsewhere.

5. Request due dates for your bills that help you stay on track and pay your bills on time.

6. Put extra money into your savings account at times when you have it.

7. Use your tax refund to help you reach your financial goals.

8. Make your meals at home. Don't eat out.

9. Shop smart. Discounts, coupons, and clearance.

10. Just say no. No to the little feel-good purchases such as Starbucks and fast fashion. Every little purchase adds up.

These are just 10 of my favorite financial health tips that you should add to your money tree and help it grow.

Stop taking shortcuts that aren't really shortcuts. Commit to changing your life and putting in the hard work it takes to get there. Take a few minutes to write down some goals you want to reach and then describe how you are going to achieve them. I know you can reach them; I have so much faith in you!

CUT YOUR EGO OFF

The ego is a tricky little bastard, and we all have one. When I think of the word ego, for me, it conjures up an image of a little macho man with an aggressive tone, a bellowing voice, and his chest puffed up. When the ego manifests itself in this way, it's obvious this person is showing up in their ego and has masked their true self. However, the ego that is not so obviously detected is the tricky little bastard we should watch out for. Often, we don't even recognize our ego and the many masks it wears, especially as women. When we first come into this world as little baby girls, we begin to be conditioned by our family, church, and society to be helpful, to be of service, to be caring, to sacrifice, to be pretty, to be polite, and to please. As much as men have been socially conditioned not to cry and to avoid their feelings and emotions by armoring up, in general, women were conditioned to keep their moral standard high and their emotional boundaries low. As women, our ego masks are much more subtle and often difficult for us to perceive within our own selves. However, even the most kind and self-aware human has a tricky little bastard frolicking around inside them, looking for ways to deceive and cut us off from the Divine Spirit and the source of who we truly are, the authentic self.

In women, ego often comes disguised as selflessness, passiveness, cheerfulness, martyrdom, and humility, just to name a few. Nobody knew that I cried in the shower every night, every single night. I was trying to maintain my household to be a good mom, a good wife, a good daughter, sibling, friend, and caregiver. I felt utterly alone. I had asked for help, and my asking only ended in disappointment and frustration, even being belittled for not being able to manage all my responsibilities. I was being crushed under the weight of my own unrealistic expectations and by the needs of my spouse as well. I felt like a complete failure. I was trying to do everything right, and yet it never seemed like I was doing anything right. I would bury my face in the washcloth or towel to muffle my sobs. Then, I would wipe my tears, get dressed, and put on my "happy" face, my "I have it all under control" face, my "I know what I'm doing" face, my "I'm good" face, and my don't worry about me, I wouldn't want to trouble you" face. I became so familiar with my many masks and hid behind so many layers of untruths that I believed my authentic self had ceased to exist. I was so cut off from the source of who I was that I no longer recognized the real joyful, spirited, and lively girl that I once was. I became who everyone needed me to be, and in the process, my ego was now in control. The ego's job is to watch out for any perceived threat to the self and convince us that we must do and become anything to stay safe. My ego self did not look like the macho man I described in the beginning. My ego was not a fighter; my ego, that tricky little bastard, convinced me it was safer to be a chameleon. So, I became one.

If there was one thing my traumas taught me, it was how to stay safe, to be hyper-vigilant, and to be aware of my audience. It wasn't always like that. I was once a highly opinionated, outspoken person until I learned that it was not safe to be so. My husband, children, and I had moved into a beautiful brand-new home in Arizona, and the landscaping was not yet complete. He was building stairs from the back deck. He asked me to help him decide how to design the stairs, and I gave him my honest opinion, possibly overexplaining my reason. He did not like my answer and told me what he was thinking would work best instead. I tried to argue in favor of my design until he started yelling and getting aggressive with his tone and language. I then backed down, hoping to avoid further escalation by agreeing with him, lying, and saying that I misunderstood what he was trying to tell me and that I thought his design made more sense. I wholeheartedly agreed with him. This was not the first time I would abandon my truth, nor would it be the last. To be fair to him, I did get the fountain I had always wanted in the front yard.

I learned to abandon my truth, my wants, and my needs. I learned to remain silent when I wanted to scream. But the biggest thing I learned was that it was not safe to be myself. So, I continued to hide behind masks instead of breaking free. Because of my ego, that tricky little bastard convinced me I wasn't safe to leave. Let me tell you that the victim mask is very comfortable. Shifting the blame and not taking responsibility for ourselves and the life we truly deserve is easy. It requires little to no effort on our part because everyone else has complete control and power over us. So, we morph ourselves, changing our image to better suit others' moods and whims, and in the process, we cut ourselves off from who we really are and why we were given a unique soul to begin with. This is how we know the ego is running the show: we are exhausted, we are confused, and we feel powerless. When we are living our authentic truth, we feel alive, confident, and empowered. With that in mind, do you know who's running the show?

If you've ever lived in a small town, you understand the importance of reputation— your individual reputation and that of your family. Growing up as a pastor's daughter, I knew firsthand the importance of reputation. My father was a man of good character; he had an established reputation, and our family was well regarded. So, when, as a single, young, unwed mother, I attended my father's church, I felt as though not only had I damaged my reputation, but I had tarnished my father's good name as well. For that, I was deeply remorseful. As you can imagine, a minister's reputation is of the utmost importance. Living in a small town is no exception. Word gets around in a small town and spreads like wildfire, and trust me, you do not want to be at the center of small-town gossip. That's where our tricky little friend, the ego, comes in handy. The ego helps us to create and maintain our image of ourselves and our reputation. For this, I suffered the most.

My image was good, and my reputation was great, as was my family's. I cared for children in my home, which I loved. All four of my children were high achievers in all aspects. I was hard on them in this regard. I was a smother mother and overprotective, not only for their physical safety but also for the safety of their reputation and our reputation. Don't get me wrong, I love that small town and the people who live there, and most of the people are so loving and wonderful, but I saw what happened to good people who made poor choices and how they were never able to recover their good reputation once it was tarnished. From the outside, people would have thought we were an average, good family. My children never got into any trouble; they were all straight A students; some were involved in sports and others in band; and they had good-quality friends. My husband was hardworking and reliable. I was considered a great mom who was involved in her children's lives. Packing their lunches every day, attending their events, school field trips, etc. The ego builds this false image and does everything it can to protect the image from breaking. The ego can convince us that the false world we have created is, in fact, real. I had convinced myself that the mistreatment I was receiving in the home by my spouse was acceptable and manageable. The repeated incidences of name-calling and aggression were normal, and all families experienced this. That physically standing between him and one of our children and him grabbing me by the forearms and dragging me down the stairs, leaving bruises, were "not that bad." On several occasions, I should have called the police. However, two things entered my mind: I didn't want to subject my children to seeing the police at our home and the possibility of seeing their dad taken away in handcuffs. What would this do to our family's reputation? So, I waited for the storm to pass, as it always did, usually after the liquor wore off. Please understand that I do not wish to shame him or make excuses for him. This is my personal account of what I experienced. I cannot tell you how I went from being cut off to being complete, from being empty to being empowered, without sharing some of the causes of the emptiness that cut me off from myself. I take full responsibility for performing the role my ego chose to entertain instead of freeing myself from a toxic situation. When we allow for this type of dynamic, we cut ourselves off from our personal power. This creates an ego mask of victimhood, a victim mentality, which is honestly just another form of self-centeredness. A martyr with a God complex is the worst. I can say this now because I am more aware of my ego self and my ego's need to please others by abandoning my truth to gain a false sense of safety. I am aware of the many masks I have hidden behind to keep myself safe. I recognize all the false personas I have put on to protect my reputation. Much of my self-reflection time is centered around removing the layers of masks I have worn over the years. It is my goal to be the complete, truest, and most authentic version of myself, always keeping in mind that the ego is a tricky little bastard.

Truly, I would love nothing more than for each of us to succeed in life, and to do that, we have to find the me behind the mask and cut the ego off. One common and destructive way our ego reveals its ugly self is by convincing us to take everything personally. It's believing that everything that happens and how other people treat us is somehow about us. When, in reality, it rarely is. In fact, the sad truth is that people think about us even less than you can imagine. Why? Because they too are mostly focused on themselves, their own emotions, and their own interests. So how can we cultivate a "cut me off mindset" and stop taking everything so personally? I think we tend to hurt our own feelings with the stories we tell ourselves. When we have an encounter with another person and they are acting "weird" with us, we tend to let our thoughts tell us a story about why that other person might be treating us differently than we were expecting. These thoughts tend to spiral into what we did wrong and often end with self-criticism and blame, as well as hurt, tense feelings towards the other person. How do we end this cycle of self-pity?

1. Recognize when it's happening.
2. Be an observer of your thoughts.
3. Make a note of the story you are telling yourself.
4. Reflect and take responsibility for your inner wound that has been triggered by this encounter. This is your lesson, and they are the teachers.
5. Remind yourself that you are the storyteller.
6. Tell a different story.
For example, "Most likely, this person's mood is not about me. I trust that if they are upset with me, they will tell me. I trust that I can handle the conversation, should it occur. It is not my job to fix or regulate another person's mood.
7. Be grateful for the opportunity to learn more about yourself and others.

8. Release the experience with love and grace.

By telling a different story, one that is usually more logical, we release ourselves and the other person from a false narrative. These assumed and typically false narratives have the power to destroy good and loving relationships. We take our power back when we take personal responsibility instead of taking everything personally. One is rooted in victimhood (ego), and the other is rooted in personal power (true self). I had traveled to Arizona to see my parents, siblings, and other family members. My husband and I had just separated, and I did not want to spend my first Mother's Day without contact with my children and my birthday without them. While on that trip, I told my family that my husband and I would be getting a divorce. I told them everything. They were sad, and it seemed like they wanted to be supportive. I did not hear from them, not even my own mother, from May to November. While I was going through the darkest days of my life, my family was MIA. To make matters worse, they knew I was distraught and suicidal over the lack of contact with my children.

By the time October and early November rolled around, you could imagine the stories I was telling myself about the lack of communication from my own family. Nobody wants me. No one cares about me. I must be a horrible person who is unworthy of love. I have been abandoned and rejected by all the people I love most, and I am the common denominator. What is so wrong with me is that my own family could treat me this way. The pity party continued. After all I've done, after all the effort I have made to be in their lives, after all, I have sacrificed for them, spiraling. I want to be very clear that if I had not been years into my personal healing journey and if it had not been for a couple earth angel friends of mine, I am not sure I could have climbed out of that pit I was in. The other thing that helped me during these dark days was that I knew better than to believe the negative thoughts that were surfacing.

Though my initial response was to armor up and become bitter and resentful, I continued the good fight, to growl back at those negative self-pitting false beliefs: "I refuse to become hard; I refuse to break under the pressure of this test; I know who I am. I stand firm in who I am. I AM LOVE! My purpose is to love—to BE love without limits or expectations. I knew the Divine Spirit had my back too, and I could feel the love of the spiritual world surrounding me in full force. It was a powerful feeling. I would be taking one of my long healing walks on the beach, and as those negative thoughts would come, it happened that I would look down at just the right moment and a heart-shaped rock, seashell, leaf, or piece of coral would be there in my path. This has been, for many years now, the Divine Spirit's way to remind me to stay on the path of love. When I see these heart shapes, it makes me aware of my thoughts and the reality my thoughts are creating, and they remind me to create love. It's important to learn to allow these false thoughts and feelings to pass through our awareness and to learn to let them go so that we can create space for new and positive thought programming to exist. Our negative thoughts do need to come to the surface to be released and replaced. It is when we continually entertain these negative thoughts and choose to embrace these thoughts as truth that we cut ourselves off from the power of love that we are here to create.

When I spoke with my mother and a few of my siblings, the story was very different from the one I had told myself. They had been thinking about me, and they did care. They simply did not know what to say. They thought about reaching out many times. They wanted to offer more support, but they didn't know how. They assumed that if I needed them, I would reach out. They wanted to respect my privacy (for context, they are all introverts; I am the only extrovert in my family). They love me very much. If I had chosen to continue believing my false stories or if I had decided to take their absence personally, I would have cut them off. I would have surrendered to bitterness and resentfulness, and I would miss out on all the loving memories that have yet to be made. I am leaving in two weeks to go spend time making more wonderful memories with them.

We tend to cut people off when we really should be cutting our egos off instead. Releasing our wounded pride and setting aside our egos allows us to embrace more of the good stuff. We were given life and, with it, all the tools to create a more abundant life. However, we must battle that tiny little inner trickster, the ego, to create the life of abundance—that life beyond our wildest good dreams. The ego self is the inner devil that has come to steal, kill, and destroy you, your relationships, your family, your body, your mind, your heart, and your soul. Searching all of the places within ourselves where the ego self is running the show and creating the narrative, then beating their ass by taking our personal power back, is the most loving thing we can do for ourselves and others. I need to remind you that love is the most powerful force on earth. I encourage you to stay on the path of love, and love will be made manifest in your life in an abundant way.

CUT TO THE CHASE

Badass bitches don't play around when it comes to creating the life of their dreams. We cut out the crap and cut to the chase. They don't chase men, money, or momentary pleasers. Badass women chase peace, purpose, and power (self-empowerment). Badass women take full responsibility for all aspects of our lives. We refuse to be victims of our circumstances and, therefore, know how to create the life we want instead of settling for the life that wants us.

Let's be clear: Badass Bitches are not mean; they are not overly aggressive; they are not rude or coldhearted. In fact, most women who are truly badass are in control of their emotions; they are fair, warm, and kind. A powerful woman is a woman who is in control of the only thing she can control: herself. Women of purpose do not play the victim, and they do not make excuses. If there is an area in their life that is not aligned with their purpose, they do not hesitate to cut it out of their life completely. They make their own decisions and accept the consequences without blaming others. They work hard but also make time for self-care and service to a higher cause.

Here's the method I used that took me from being cut off from myself (feeling empty) to being complete (feeling empowered).

How a former people-pleasing pussy became the empowered badass bitch she is today.

How to Build a Badass Bitch:

Prioritize yourself.

Practice saying "no."

Ask for help.

Boost your self-confidence.

Stop comparing and competing by focusing on what creates you. Read and listen to empowering books and podcasts.

Lovingly evaluate the people, situations, and things in your life and add or eliminate them accordingly.

Exercise and eat nutritional foods.

Smile.

Spend time connecting to nature.

Speak affirming words to yourself.

Express gratitude.

Meditation.

Have spiritual practices.

Fully embrace your body and sexuality.

Be bold in your authenticity.

Look for reasons to be happy and see the positive in all situations, people, and experiences.

Invest in adventure, play, and fun.

Practice living in the power of the moment. We create our lives in the now.

Be ambitious, enthusiastic, and passionate about the life you are consciously creating.

Have a vision for the future, but be flexible with how you'll get there.

Show up now like you are the future version of yourself.

Surround yourself with inspiring people.

A badass creates herself and the life she knows she deserves. She loves herself enough to cut the crap and chase the life of her dreams. When I was in high school, I had a friend who did not have an ideal home life. Her parents were divorced, she had little to no contact with her father, her mother struggled with substance abuse, and many men were in and out of the home (if you know what I mean). According to statistics, based on her home life and life experiences, she should have followed in her mother's footsteps. However, she did not, and I remember watching the moment she said no to that path and began to transform into something and someone entirely different, and I will never forget it. First, she started coming to school dressed like a businesswoman. She wore blazers, skirts, pantyhose, and dress shoes. Shortly after, she got a job at a high-end department store. She began to carry herself with the utmost dignity and self-respect. We started having lunch in the library, where even our conversations were different. I admired her and the transformation she was going through. She was dating a mutual friend, and I also began to see a positive change in him as well. After high school, she was one of the few friends I kept in touch with. She went on to be a very successful businesswoman who balanced both a thriving career and a beautiful family that she created with our mutual friend and her high school sweetheart. As I reflect on witnessing the beginning of her transformation, the biggest takeaway for me is that she showed up as a woman she admired long before she had fully grown into that role. She had a vision for her life, and her dedication and consistency to this higher version of herself made it possible. I am inspired by her courage. Getting dressed up neatly in a messy environment, walking out of the door of poverty with dignity, going to school dressed like a successful adult, and coming back home, only to do it on repeat. She had a vision for her future, she was determined to succeed, she was focused, and she worked her ass off. She did not make excuses or repeat a family cycle. Cycle breakers are some of the most brave and admirable humans I know. She still has her warm smile and kind, caring soul. She taught me to show up as the version of myself I want to be and to never give up on my goals and dreams, no excuses. We must be determined, consistent, and fearless in the pursuit of the best, most badass version of ourselves. If we cut the bullshit limiting beliefs from our thoughts and have a vision for the best version of ourselves, I believe we can achieve the unimaginable.

I am writing this chapter as I sit at my kitchen table by a window with a view of the ocean. My life looks completely different from the life I had before. Before, I lived in my dream five-bedroom farmhouse. I raised my family in a small, midwestern town. Now I am raising myself. After a lifetime of nurturing others, sadly, I am an unhealed human. I am nurturing that human who I needed to look after the most. The healing journey is messy and lonely, but if we can look for good in all things, it will not only help, but we will see beauty all around us and in all things. I won't forget the moment I walked the narrow, sandy path that led to the view of the ocean. You know that feeling? When we first see the massive churning waters of the ocean, we feel a sense of awe. I knew I was home. I had asked for this life, in a way. I was tired of feeling empty and cut off from myself. I gave up a large part of myself, my happiness, and my dreams to raise a family. Do I regret it? Absolutely not. I regret how I was and the way I managed many things throughout those years. But I tried; I made sacrifices, as we all do. I raised four beautiful children that I love and will always love with all my heart. However, they are adults now and must make their own way in the world as I must continue my journey. I could have chosen to stay in a place where I felt I did not belong, but I chose instead to keep growing and expanding. I aspire to live a life of awe and wonder. I aspire to walk on this path of life, to have the views and experiences that take my breath away. I asked for this life when I realized I wanted a bigger life. I went for a walk in one of my sacred nature places, and I said to the Divine Spirit, "I want to live a life beyond my wildest good dreams." I then went into specifics and now have many of the things I requested, including a view of the ocean. I cut to the chase with my life, I got real, and I owned what it was that I truly wanted. I accepted that, at 50, I still had a lot of life left to live and that I was going to make it a big life. A big love life. I am in the middle of my story, and I believe some of my best and biggest moments are yet to come.

I believe when we begin to cut to the chase and get real with who we want to be and who we want to become, the Divine Spirit will conspire to make it all happen for us. No matter how big. Keeping in mind that all things come at a cost.

I had gone to the tree park half a block from my beach condo (I also asked for a tree park because I love trees), and I was sitting on the exposed roots of the tree with my back leaned up against the tree, crying and talking to the Divine Spirit. Saying how difficult this journey is and how, admittedly, sometimes I wish that I was content to live a quiet, tucked-away life. I wished that I was someone else or had a different purpose. I was feeling a bit sorry for myself, forgetting how fortunate I am and all that has been granted to me. I was longing for my old, familiar life. Spirit broke through my sadness, reminding me that living a life beyond my wildest good dreams comes with a price. I must release the old self and old life to fully embrace this new one. We cannot be who we were, do what we used to do, and expect to live a new life. I had already transformed into a better version of myself, and much like a butterfly who cannot return to her cocoon, I could not return to my former self and my former life, even if I had moments when I wanted to.

Once we accept that the old us has transformed into something new, something more, we are free. We release the weight of yesterday and begin to soar. I decided that the suffering of remaining the same and in the same relationship dynamics was a greater price to pay than the unknown. If I may encourage you, when you see what is waiting for you at the end of this unknown, you will be in awe of the view. If you stay on the journey, if you cut to the chase, the pursuit of you and your dreams, you will be greeted with the most miraculous moments and experiences. You will see how loved and cared for you are by the creator. Everything unfolds in perfect timing as you trust that you are in faithful hands.
I followed the steps I mentioned at the beginning of the chapter to create this peaceful, purposeful, and powerful version of me. Once I felt a stirring in my soul to transform myself and my life, I began with my body. Why

begin with the body? We need to feel physically strong and have the energy to create our dream person. I started by taking responsibility for my diet and exercise. I became a vegan. Eating plant based food, mostly fresh fruits and vegetables, made me feel better. It gave me more energy and focus. By choosing to eat this way, I gained the energy and confidence to start exercising. Being vegan transformed me in other ways as well. I became more interested in yoga and meditation. When I chose to go vegan, originally, I was only going to try it for one week (as a challenge for myself). After one week, I felt so amazed that I continued my journey. I think that becoming a vegan for a few years was a way for my body, mind, and spirit to purge food toxins from my body. The process of purging these physical toxins from my body positively affected my mental health. And when I added yoga and meditation to my routine, my emotional wellbeing became healthier too. This is where it all began for me. Once we feel better physically, we open our awareness to other areas of our lives that could use a bit of an upgrade. Not only did I feel great, but I was looking better too. I lost over 40 pounds, and my youthful appearance and that healthy glow returned. During this time, I added affirmations to my daily routine. My body was working with my mind, and I started to believe that I was worthy. Once we know our worth, it's game over for anyone and anything that does not treat us accordingly. It's a process; it's a lot of work, but it can be fun work. Work that is worth the effort because we are worth the effort.

Cutting to the chase! Who do you want to become? What is it you want to do? What is your vision for the future? Start chasing that version of you now. Begin by being honest with yourself, and begin cutting out the old people and things that do not feel like the version of yourself that you are creating. Be ruthless with your time and energy. Say no when you mean "no" so that you can create space to say yes to the things that make you feel excited. Speaking of excitement, we have got to get enthusiastic and passionate about creating our lives. This is our story, after all. When we stop living for the approval of others and step into our most peaceful, purposeful, and powerful selves, we are in creation mode. The more we embody this evolution and show up as this higher version of ourselves, the more confident we become. The more confident we become, the more we step into our new reality and the life beyond our wildest good dreams. You can be and achieve anything you put your thoughts and actions to. Chase your dreams, pursue your goals... You, badass goal-getter!

LOVE IN THE CUT

Love in the cut (a relationship that occurs from an unlikely origin and between two people from very different backgrounds that hook up for the long term)

It's 3:33, and I just got off the airplane. I was relieved to make it back home with no flight delays or issues. I was gone for 24 hours. He booked and paid for an expensive plane ticket for one night. We met at an upscale hotel, and we enjoyed drinks at the bar and fine dining together. We can talk about everything and anything. We speak openly and freely with each other. We flirt, touch, and tease until the sexual tension builds, and when neither of us can control our desires, we go to the beautiful hotel suite he booked for the night. He is generous in every way and makes me feel desired and special. He is attractive, wealthy, and a man of importance. Being with him is like being in another world, leaving my humdrum life and entering a fairytale. It's a fantasy, I know.

The final chapter of this book is where it all began. It is where I explain how love saved me. It is the love story of a lifetime. I once wished for a love like this. I would wish that I could live and experience the greatest love story ever told, and I did.

There are choices that we make every day that, in the moment, seem ordinary. It is not until further reflection that we realize how one single simple decision—like what doorway to cross through—will change the course of our entire existence.

There I was, standing in a crowded banquet hall between two doors. For a moment in time, I had a simple decision to make: to exit from the door closest to me or to choose the other door across from me. If I had walked out of the door, I had intended to walk out for practical reasons, and I would have walked back to my familiar life. I have no doubt I would still be married to my husband, living in my old house, working the same job, and living the same mundane and comfortable life. However, I did not exit from the door that was closest or most convenient. I chose instead to walk across the dance floor. I stayed to meet the people who had been honored that evening and crossed through the "other" door. This door would lead me to the greatest love story I've ever known or could have even imagined.

The first time I saw him, I recognized him. Well, I recognized something about him. He was speaking, wearing a finely tailored suit, well-groomed, and very attractive. I remember feeling sick; I had tunnel vision, and all the noises around me seemed to fade. It was like I was watching myself, and everything was in slow motion. I had never experienced anything like that. I don't believe in love at first sight; that's ridiculous. I am a very practical person. To this day, I refuse to admit that love at first sight exists; however, I decided that if love at first sight did exist, it must feel as awful and scary as that moment. He had such a sincere, humble, and kind way about him. He spoke so authentically, and his genuine nature made him more charming to me than any man I had ever known. I thought to myself, a thought that would occur many times that night, "I know him from somewhere." After he was done speaking or during, I don't remember, I took out my phone and started googling what movies he had been in. When I did not find any movies, I googled what TV show he was in; we'll call him A Unicorn. When I found that my Google search of his name yielded nothing of obvious importance, I put my phone away. Yet the question persisted: "How do I know him?" I saw the people honored being interviewed, and although I did not know them, I thought it might be nice to meet someone who is as incredible as them, and additionally, I thought I would have an interesting story to tell about meeting these famous people.

As I was waiting to meet them, the gentleman I had mentioned earlier (that I was sure I recognized) approached me. I felt a wave of nausea hit me so hard that I wanted to run. It didn't help that he looked a bit stern and serious as he approached, and I thought I might be getting into trouble for taking pictures of his clients while they were being interviewed. Did I mention I was taking pictures when I probably wasn't supposed to? I still remember the feeling of his breath on the side of my face when he leaned in to speak over the loud music so that I could hear him. "Do you want to meet them?" He spoke. I was extremely nervous. I stammered all over my words and said too much, explaining that I had no idea who they were, but since I'm here, I might as well meet them. "Besides," I said, one of my children is into this thing, and they might think it's cool. I ramble. I ramble when I am nervous, obviously. While waiting to meet them, I studied his face repeatedly, and I asked the question quietly to my innermost self, "How do I know you?"

Imagine my surprise when a voice answered back, "You know him from past lives." Naturally, my immediate response was an internal laugh followed by "girl, we don't believe in that." As I mentioned before, my religious indoctrination would not allow me to consider such a thing. This very simple thought, "You know him from past lives," would open a whole new reality, one that I had always doubted and feared. "Is it possible we have lived many lives?" I have pondered this question. I have studied. I have searched for answers. I have come to no definitive conclusion. All that I know with certainty is how I feel. I feel comfortable, like I've known them my whole life or many lives. I feel most at home with them. I feel safe. I trust. The first time we kissed, time stood still. I realize that sounds utterly ridiculous. I remember nothing of an elevator ride up 14 floors. Nothing. I remember our lips touching, our breaths meeting, and then I remember the elevator door opening. There have been many strange and unexplainable phenomena with regards to our connection. Like knowing when the other is in a state of high emotional discomfort without being in contact. I feel I must explain how this connection is different from anything I've ever experienced. Not to make excuses, but simply as an attempt to try to explain the unexplainable. In all the years that I have known him, not a day has gone by that I have not considered this strange connection.

I will never believe in coincidences again. I will never believe that anything is random. I will forever believe that the Divine Spirit is guiding us to people, places, and things who are meant to show, teach, and grow us along our journey. We became friends; we became more than friends. I am not proud of what I have done, but I'm not ashamed of it either. The way I see it, it was a necessary part of my evolution. Don't get me wrong; I am in no way recommending having a secret sexual affair. This is social suicide and may undermine and ruin my credibility up to this point. But I am determined to be candid and give a voice to the many women who can relate to an extramarital affair, as there are a growing number of us. I will spare you the excuses for what led to the experience. I have a whole list of excuses, ranging from my childhood traumas to a midlife crisis. But all excuses are the same, and no excuse is good enough to justify an affair of any kind. Nor will I speak of the perspective of the "other" man. I have no idea how he feels. I could have written this book without this chapter, but it would not have been complete, as this connection was the catalyst for my transformations and the reason I cut my bangs to begin with.

The catalyst for our growth can be many different things and take many different forms. These types of life-altering connections will cut you to the bone. Remove every layer of falsehood and force you to see every inch of yourself. Every naked truth. Just how far we are willing to go to find ourselves. I know at this point many of you are thinking, "I would never go this far." I understand. Despise me if you must. I hope that you will not. I am just a human woman trying to be better and do better, and this is part of my journey and my honest confession. We are all flawed. Being willing to embrace those flaws and learning from our humanity is what makes us "flawsome." Don't be ashamed to tell your story, even if it doesn't paint you in the most beautiful light. We learn best not from other successes but from the struggles, the failures, and the darkness they have overcome.

The dirty little details that should follow are for another book at another time. As for this love story, it is of little importance. What matters is what happened to me. This encounter was so impactful that I would never see myself or the world around me the same again. I've heard people in the spiritual community call this sudden change within oneself an awakening. I suppose that's what it would feel like too if someone poured a cup of ice-cold water on you and shocked you awake. It was that startling. It was as if overnight I had unlocked an entirely different level of myself and of my life in general. Suddenly, I saw beyond the life I was living and saw the life I was meant to be living. Without his knowledge, this man, whom we'll call a unicorn, was teaching me how to love myself. With every encounter and interaction, he showed me how beautiful and worthy I was. Through his inaction and lack of communication, I became aware of my wounds and began to heal them. I learned to give myself what I was lacking from him and others. I started pouring into myself, and I began to believe I deserved to give myself all the love that no one else could give me. That I could love myself the way that I had always longed to be loved. I became my own best friend and the greatest love of my own life. Now, looking for love in all the wrong places is just a worn-out, old song. My desperate need for love and validation from others outside of myself has been cut away from my soul, and I am free. The emptiness and void I used to feel have been replaced with a divine, empowering love I never thought possible. Whitney Houston sang it best: "I found the greatest love of all, inside of me."

BIG love, Bitches, from my FLAWesome full heart to yours!
-Rebecca

DEDICATION

To all my best bitches (you know who you are),

Thank you for inspiring me to write this book.
Thank you for sharing your light on my darkest
days. Because of you, I not only survived but I
thrived. You will forever have my loyalty and
love.
BIG bestie love from me to y'all

Unicorn,
Because I once captured your gaze; there in
your eyes I saw a reflection of myself and of my
own greatness. For this alone you will have my
undying gratitude and lifelong affection.

Yours truly
- Rebecca

ABOUT THE AUTHOR:

Rebecca recently moved after divorcing her husband of 30 years. Trading in her snow boots and small-town roots, for the sun and sandy beaches of Virginia. Here, she enjoys writing, sewing, and long walks on the beach.

This is Rebecca's fourth published book. Her first three books are children's books. She is passionate about stories. She enjoys sharing her stories, reading, and hearing the stories of others. She would like to encourage everyone to write about and share their personal life experiences. She firmly believes everyone has a story to share and valuable wisdom to impart. Our lives are our greatest stories, and this story has been told. The rest is still unwritten.